Cotswold Guide 2024

Discover the Cotswolds: Comprehensive 2024 Edition Unveiling Hidden Size Gems, Countryside Charm, Jewelry Cubes, and Oxford & Bath Adventures

Rick Paul

© Copyright Rick Paul 2024

All rights reserved. No part of this publication may be reproduced, distributed, or transmitted in any form or by any means, including photocopying, recording, or other electronic or mechanical methods, without the prior written permission of the publisher, except in the case of brief quotations embodied in critical reviews and certain other noncommercial uses permitted by copyright law.

Disclaimer Notice

The information in this document is for educational and entertainment purposes only. No warranties, explicit or implied, are made. The author is not providing legal, financial, medical, or professional advice. Consult licensed professionals for guidance before implementing any techniques. The author is not liable for any losses or damages resulting from the use of this information. By accessing and reading this document, the reader agrees to hold the author harmless from any direct or indirect losses or damages resulting from the use of the information provided herein. The author shall not be held liable for errors, omissions, or inaccuracies present in the content. Each reader is solely responsible for the decisions they make based on the information presented in this document.

Discovering England's Countryside

Nestled in the heart of the Cotswolds, I embarked on a journey that forever altered my perception of travel. Wandering through the cobblestone streets of Bourton-on-the-Water, basking in the grandeur of Blenheim Palace, and reveling in the timeless charm of Bibury, I discovered a world straight from the pages of a storybook.

My Cotswolds experience transcended mere beauty and history; it was an immersion into the soul of this English countryside. It involved meadows awash with wildflowers, traditional pub lunches, and the warmth of the locals.

Amidst this captivating backdrop, a burning desire took root within me: to share my Cotswolds journey with the world. I longed to connect fellow travelers with the Cotswolds' hidden treasures and its people's hospitality.

Within the pages of this book, I seek to convey the Cotswolds' enchantment – the sensation of time travel, the excitement of unspoiled landscapes, and the delight of local cuisine. I hope that, through my words and insights, others can uncover their own slice of Cotswolds paradise, creating an unforgettable adventure of their own. Join me as we unveil the Cotswolds' secrets, celebrate its timeless allure, and provide a roadmap for an extraordinary experience.

Contents

Sunset Chronicles – An Algarve Odyssey	**2**
Introduction	**8**
1.1 Cotswolds Region Overview	12
1.2 Highlights of Geography	17
1.3 Historical Importance	21
Making Travel Plans	**26**
2.1 When Is the Best Time to Visit?	26
2.3 Choosing a Place to Stay	34
2.3.1 Inns and Hotels	35
2.3.2 Hotels with Bed and Breakfast	39
2.3.3 Self-Contained Cottages	43
2.3.4 Budget-Friendly Alternatives	47
2.4 Transportation Suggestions	51
2.4.1 How to Get to the Cotswolds	52
2.4.2 Region Wide Public Transportation	56
2.4.3 Automobile Rentals and Driving	60
2.4.4 Cycling Routes and Bike Rentals	63
Top Attractions in the Cotswolds	**68**
3.1 Historic Villages and Towns	68
3.1.1 Bourton-on-the-Water	68
3.1.2 Stow-on-the-Wold	73
3.1.3 Bibury	77
3.1.4 Broadway	81
3.2 Stately Homes and Castles	90
3.2.1 Blenheim Palace	90
3.2.2 Sudeley Castle	94
3.2.3 Berkeley Castle	99
3.3 Natural Landscapes	103
3.3.1 Cotswold Hills and Scenic Walks	103

3.3.2 Cotswold Wildlife and Nature Reserves	108
3.3.3 Exploring Cotswold Water Park	112
3.4 Arts and Culture	116
3.4.1 Museums and Galleries	116
3.4.2 Performing Arts Venues	122
3.4.3 Local Artisan Shops and Studios	126
Outdoor Recreation	**131**
4.1 Trails for Hiking and Walking	131
4.1.1 National Trail of the Cotswolds	131
4.2 Cycling Routes	141
4.2.2 Difficult Cycling Routes for Enthusiasts	145
4.3 Equestrian and Horse Riding Experiences	149
4.4 Hot Air Balloon Rides	153
4.5 Golf Courses in Beautiful Locations	159
Local Dining and Cuisine	**164**
5.1 Cotswold Cuisine Overview	164
5.2 Traditional Public Houses and Gastropubs	168
5.3 Restaurants Serving Fine Dining	172
5.4 Teahouses and Cafés	176
5.5 Farmers' Markets and Local Produce	180
The Cotswolds are a great place to go shopping.	**184**
6.1 Souvenirs and Local Crafts	184
6.2 Antiques & Vintage Shops	187
6.3 Fashion Boutiques	191
6.4 Artisan Food and Drink Products	195
Events and Festivals	**199**
7.1 Cotswold Calendar of Events	199
7.2 Seasonal Celebrations	203
7.2.1 Cotswold Olympiads	203
7.2.2 Christmas Markets and Events	207
7.3 Festivals of Music and the Arts	210
7.4 Literary and Cultural Activities	214

Useful Information   **219**

8.1 Medical Facilities and Emergency Contacts   219

8.2 Banking and Currency Services   222

8.3 Internet and Communication Services   226

8.4 Language and Cultural Practices   229

8.5 Special Needs Travelers' Accessibility   232

Itineraries Examples   **243**

10.1 Itinerary for a Weekend Getaway   243

10.2 Week-Long Excursions   246

10.3 Activities for the Whole Family   250

Travel and Photography Tips   **255**

11.1 Capturing the Beauty of the Cotswolds   255

11.2 Travel Photography Practices That Are Respectful   259

11.3 Ideas for a Memorable Cotswolds Vacation   263

Introduction

Discovering England's Timeless Jewel

Welcome to the Cotswolds, a region that appears to have arisen from the pages of a fairy tale. The Cotswolds, located in the heart of England, is a patchwork of natural beauty, historical significance, and quaint villages that invite you to enter a world that is both timeless and captivating. Allow us to be your guide as you begin your adventure through this region, uncovering the mysteries and beauties that the Cotswolds have to offer.

A Sight of Unspoiled Beauty

Consider a scene of serene majesty, with rolling hills covered with lush meadows and crisscrossed by meandering streams and age-old stone walls. This is the Cotswolds, a six-county area of around 800 square miles that offers a retreat from the hectic pace of modern life. Each village and town appears to have been taken from a fairy tale, with honey-colored buildings and cobblestone streets creating a lovely and friendly ambience.

Discovering Timeless Treasures

The Cotswolds are more than just a beautiful location; they are also a living witness to millennia of history. As you travel through the meandering alleys, you'll come across settlements that formerly flourished in the medieval wool trade, as evidenced by the spectacular structures that dot the countryside. Majestic churches, elegant manor residences, and timber-framed structures are quiet memorials to a bygone era. You'll feel as if you've gone back in time as you discover these treasures, connecting with the stories of people who traveled these routes before you.

Exploring the Cotswolds

Each village in the Cotswolds has its own distinct character. In Bourton-on-the-Water, sometimes known as the "Venice of the Cotswolds," peaceful streams run beneath low stone bridges, creating a landscape of unparalleled serenity. Stow-on-the-Wold, with its bustling market area, welcomes you to indulge in the pleasures of traditional market towns. Bibury is famous for its

Arlington Row, a row of centuries-old weaver's homes that has appeared on innumerable postcards.

A Natural Splendor Tapestry

The Cotswolds offer a canvas of natural beauty that is as diverse as it is compelling outside of the towns. Your activities will be set against the backdrop of the Cotswold Hills, a series of mild slopes. Explore the Cotswold Way National Trail on foot, soaking in the fresh air and marveling at the panoramic views. The region's woodlands and nature parks are home to a diverse range of species, from deer to rare birds, providing a haven of discovery for nature enthusiasts.

Taking on the Cotswold Way of Life

Time appears to slow down in the Cotswolds, inviting you to relish life's simple pleasures. Imagine yourself sipping afternoon tea in a gorgeous tearoom, the clink of china cups creating a soothing melody. Wander through local markets and shops, where artists display their wares and farmers sell fresh produce from the region's fertile grounds.

Engage with residents whose kindness and generosity make you feel like a welcomed friend, encapsulating the Cotswold way of life.

Your journey awaits you.

Allow the appeal of this region's history, beauty, and charm to captivate your senses as you embark on your Cotswolds tour. The Cotswolds offers an experience that will linger with you long after you've returned home, whether you're meandering down centuries-old streets, catching the colors of the landscape through your camera lens, or simply taking in the tranquillity of the countryside. This guide is your key to unlocking the treasures of the Cotswolds, guiding you through every step of your journey and ensuring that you create memories to last a lifetime.

Prepare to be an enchanted, lovely traveler. The Cotswolds await your discovery, ready to offer its timeless tales and hidden gems as you embark on an experience that will have a special place in your heart for the rest of your life.

I hope this thorough introduction reflects the essence of the Cotswolds and lays the stage for any traveler to have a great vacation. Please let me know if you have any additional sections you'd like to investigate!

1.1 Cotswolds Region Overview

Welcome to the Cotswolds, a land of timeless beauty and enticing charm that invites you to go on a journey through one of England's most treasured regions. The Cotswolds, which cover six counties and approximately 800 square miles, contain a patchwork of landscapes, villages, and cultural treasures that have enticed visitors for years. In this area, we invite you to delve into the heart of the Cotswolds, discovering what makes this region so special and why it continues to captivate visitors.

A Land of Exciting Contrasts

The Cotswolds are a study in contrasts, a harmonic mix of natural and man-made beauty. The Cotswold Hills, an undulating stretch that lends the area its name, are located in the center of this region. Although the hills themselves are not towering giants, their gentle slopes and undulating curves provide a magnificent canvas for exploration. These hills, which are blanketed in lush pastures, are a tapestry of colors that change with the seasons, from vivid greens in the spring and summer to rich golds and reds in the fall.

A Trip Through Time

The Cotswolds have witnessed the passage of centuries and proudly wear the markings of their historical significance. The area developed during the Middle Ages, propelled by the wool trade. The wealth generated by this trade can be seen in the architecture that adorns the landscape. The Cotswolds are a treasure trove of limestone villages with time-honored homes with steep roofs and mullioned windows that demonstrate the affluence of centuries ago. You'll sense a connection to individuals who once lived in these communities as you traverse the cobblestone streets.

Beautiful Villages Stuck in Time

The Cotswolds are renowned with traditional English towns that appear to be frozen in time. Consider Bibury, where Arlington Row, a row of 17th-century weaver's homes, is a symbol of Cotswold charm. With its peaceful streams and low bridges, Bourton-on-the-Water has earned the nickname "Venice of the Cotswolds." Stow-on-the-Wold, set on a hill, has a bustling market square and medieval market cross, tempting you to walk into its vivid past.

Cultural and artistic wealth

The Cotswolds are more than simply natural beauty and charming houses; they are also a cultural and artistic sanctuary. Throughout the region, there is a thriving arts culture with galleries presenting both local and international talent. Museums provide insight into the region's history, especially the interesting world of the wool trade. The theatrical arts thrive here as well, with theaters and venues hosting a variety of performances that represent the town's broad interests.

A Paradise for Outdoor Enthusiasts

The Cotswolds are a playground of alternatives for individuals who enjoy the natural outdoors. The Cotswold Way National Trail, which stretches for more than 100 miles, is a refuge for walkers and ramblers. Immerse yourself in the scenery as you travel through hills, woods, and valleys, stopping for panoramic vistas along the way. Cyclists can enjoy the pleasures of cantering through meadows and along historic bridleways, while horseback riders can enjoy the pleasures of cantering through meadows and along ancient bridleways.

Embracing the Cotswold Way of Life

The Cotswolds are more than a destination; they are a way of life that encourages you to pause, taste, and connect. Tea houses and pubs offer a look into this rhythm, encouraging you to indulge in afternoon tea or a pint of locally brewed ale. Markets and fairs highlight local crafts and produce, allowing you to interact with the community while also bringing a piece of the Cotswold spirit home with you.

Your Adventure Is Awaiting You

When you enter the Cotswolds, you embark on an experience that spans time and space. The Cotswolds provide an escape into a realm of tranquillity and beauty, where each town has a tale to tell and each landscape makes a picture. This guide is your companion, designed to guide you through this magical region, ensuring that every element of your vacation, from planning to exploring, is seamless and wonderful.

Prepare to be charmed, lovely travelers. The Cotswolds are eager to reveal their treasures to you, providing an unforgettable experience for your heart and soul. The Cotswolds welcome you with open arms to discover their secrets, embrace their beauty, and make experiences that will last a lifetime.

1.2 Highlights of Geography

Welcome to the Cotswolds' geographic heart, a region that provides a breathtaking portrayal of nature's magnificence and diversity. This section will introduce you to the stunning landscapes, compelling landmarks, and distinctive geographical features that define the Cotswolds. Each highlight, from rolling hills to peaceful streams, adds to the region's undeniable beauty. Let us embark on an adventure as we delve into the geographical wonders that make the Cotswolds a true natural masterpiece.

The Gentle Elegance of the Cotswold Hills

The Cotswold Hills are the most distinguishing feature of the Cotswolds. These hills are distinguished by their gentle slopes and undulating curves rather than by their towering peaks. Their allure comes not from their grandeur, but from their graceful embracing of the surroundings. The hills create a lovely backdrop to your Cotswolds experience, with a constantly changing palette of colors that change with the seasons. The hills provide a visual feast that is a photographer's dream, whether it's the vivid greens of spring, the golden hues of summer, or the flaming reds of October.

Beautiful Valleys and Meadows

Among the hills are gorgeous valleys and meadows straight out of a pastoral painting. The Cotswolds are crisscrossed with streams that meander through the valleys, adding to the tranquillity of the landscape. As you walk along the pathways, you'll be surrounded by beautiful vegetation, wildflowers, and possibly even grazing sheep. These valleys provide a peaceful respite from the outside world, inviting you to take a moment to appreciate the natural beauty that surrounds you.

Nature's Playground: Cotswold Water Park

Dive into a world of aquatic beauty at the Cotswold Water Park, a collection of over 150 lakes that provide a home for both water enthusiasts and wildlife. This vast network of lakes provides a variety of sports, including kayaking and paddleboarding, as well as fishing and birdwatching. During the warmer months, the lakes glitter in the sun, beckoning you to partake in water-based sports and relax in the peace and quiet of the surroundings.

Nature Reserves and Ancient Woodlands

The Cotswolds are home to a treasure trove of ancient woodlands and natural reserves, where a symphony of rustling leaves, chirping birds, and wind whispers create an immersive experience. These reserves are home to a variety of flora and fauna, including deer, owls, and unique butterflies. Whether you take guided hikes in the woods or simply find a quiet space to connect with nature, you'll discover peace and amazement in these tranquil nooks.

The National Trail of the Cotswolds: Panoramic Views

The Cotswold Way National Trail attracts visitors looking for a walking experience, promising breathtaking views and adventurous treks. The trail winds its way through the Cotswold Hills for nearly 100 miles, providing stunning views at every turn. Whether you take a leisurely stroll or a more strenuous hike, the Cotswold Way offers a unique opportunity to immerse yourself in the region's natural splendor while testing your adventurous spirit.

Seasonal Symphony

One of the most enthralling aspects about the Cotswolds is how it changes with the seasons. Witness nature's rebirth in spring, when blossoms adorn the trees and fields bloom. Summer floods the environment with sunlight, beckoning you to explore its broad spaces and bask in its warmth. Autumn delivers a kaleidoscope of hues as trees and leaves transform into a stunning mosaic of reds, oranges, and golds. Even in the dead of winter, with its crisp air and snug atmosphere, there is a different kind of beauty that captures the heart.

A Wonderful World Awaits

As you travel across the geographical features of the Cotswolds, you will encounter a world that is as diverse as it is compelling. The Cotswolds' geographical features, from the gentle embrace of the hills to the tranquillity of the streams, invite you to connect with nature and find inspiration in its ever-changing canvas. Whether you're an ardent hiker, a nature lover, or simply looking for some peace and quiet, the Cotswolds provide a setting in which you can immerse yourself in the natural world's treasures.

1.3 Historical Importance

Welcome to a time travel adventure in the Cotswolds, where history is woven into the very fabric of the terrain. As you explore this area, you will find the stories that have fashioned the Cotswolds into the magical paradise that it is today. From medieval wealth to architectural marvels, the Cotswolds' historical significance is a tapestry that invites you to enter a world of intrigue and curiosity.

The Medieval Wool Trade: A Prosperity Driver

The history of the Cotswolds begins with the medieval wool trade, which pushed the region into extraordinary prosperity. The rolling hills and rich valleys were excellent for sheep rearing, and the high-quality wool produced here quickly became a sought-after product throughout Europe. The wealth generated by this trade left a lasting impression on the environment, influencing the architecture and character of the Cotswold communities.

Architecture Stuck in Time

When you visit the villages and towns of the Cotswolds, you'll find a treasure trove of architectural masterpieces dating back centuries. The honey-colored limestone homes, many of which date back to the 15th and 16th centuries, demonstrate the profitability of the wool trade. Explore the cobblestone alleys lined with timber-framed cottages to discover the secrets buried within their walls. Churches, too, are architectural marvels, with their massive spires and elaborate carvings providing a look into the region's spiritual and cultural legacy.

The Silk Road and Market Towns

The Cotswolds flourished as trade routes expanded and developed. Market towns like Stow-on-the-Wold and Moreton-in-Marsh grew into bustling commercial centers, attracting traders from all over the country. The "Silk Road" of the Cotswolds, so named because of its prominence in the wool and silk trade, connected the area to the rest of England and beyond. Today, remnants of this old trading network can be found in the market squares and market crosses that dot these cities.

Tudor ancestry and royal ties

The historical fabric of the Cotswolds stretches into the Tudor period, a period of cultural and architectural significance. Notable Tudor constructions, such as the famed Anne Hathaway's Cottage, reveal details about historical people's lives. Furthermore, the Cotswolds have close ties to British nobility. Sudeley Castle, previously home to Katherine Parr, King Henry VIII's sixth wife, is a testimony to the region's royal connections.

Keeping the Past Alive for Future Generations

The people of the Cotswolds have shown a strong commitment to conserving their historical heritage. Organizations and societies have worked valiantly to preserve the area's architectural gems and cultural histories. Museums, such as Cirencester's Corinium Museum, offer a glimpse into the past by presenting objects that recount the stories of previous generations. By participating in these activities, you contribute to the continuous preservation of the Cotswolds' ancient legacy.

Immersion into Living History

You're not just sightseeing as you walk down the cobblestone streets and see the historic structures; you're immersing yourself in living history. Shepherds, traders, artists, and royals' stories resonate through the years, inviting you to connect with the past in a truly intimate way. The Cotswolds offer a profound and authentic tour through the annals of time, whether you're staring at the beautiful carvings on a church front or visualizing the bustling markets of yesteryear.

Making Your Own Historical Chapter

As you learn about the historical significance of the Cotswolds, you become a participant in a story that is still unfolding. Your footfall mirrors those of countless others who have left their imprint on this land. Your visit to the Cotswolds adds to the rich tapestry of experiences that characterize this region. Accept the role of the modern traveler, ready to learn, share, and write your own chapter in the Cotswolds' continuous tale.

Making Travel Plans

Welcome to the "Planning Your Trip" section, where the adventure begins before you even arrive in the Cotswolds. This chapter serves as your guidebook, walking you through the fundamental parts of creating an amazing trip in this enchanting place. This chapter is your arsenal for making a seamless and enjoyable Cotswolds vacation, from picking when to visit to selecting the appropriate accommodation, knowing transit options, and even planning for outdoor adventures. So, let us begin the voyage of planning that will provide the groundwork for your discovery of this timeless region.

2.1 When Is the Best Time to Visit?

Choosing the best time to visit the Cotswolds can influence your entire experience, as each season bestows this region with its own distinct charm and attraction. In this section, we'll walk you through the nuances of each season so you can make an informed decision depending on your preferences and interests. Whether you're drawn to the exuberance of spring, the leisurely days of summer, the creative palette of fall, or the cozy embrace of winter, your trip through the Cotswolds is sure to be a sensory experience.

Nature Awakens in Spring

The Cotswolds come alive with the bright vitality of spring as winter's grip loosens. From March to May, the landscape transforms into a kaleidoscope of colors. Daffodils, tulips, and cherry blossoms create a symphony of blooms in the towns and countryside. The air is crisp and refreshing, making it an excellent time for outdoor activity. Take leisurely strolls through wildflower-adorned fields, hike along the Cotswold Way National Trail, and immerse yourself in nature's unfolding visual feast.

Summertime: Sunshine and Peace

The Cotswolds bask in the warm embrace of summer from June through August. The days are long, and the light adds a golden glow to the countryside. Festivals, fairs, and outdoor events bring the spirit of the season to life in villages. It's the ideal season for unhurried exploration, whether you're strolling through lively markets, having picnics by quiet streams, or tasting the flavors of local cuisine at open-air cafes. With its appealing lakes, the Cotswold Water Park welcomes you to paddle, swim, or simply relax on its shores.

Autumn: A Colorful Tapestry

From September to November, the Cotswolds transforms into a work of art of reds, oranges, and golds. The changing leaves adorn the hills and woodlands, producing a landscape that is nothing short of magnificent. This is the season for beauty enthusiasts—photographers, artists, and anybody who delights in the interplay of light and color. Take picturesque drives to catch the essence of fall, or explore the Cotswold wildlife and nature reserves, where the rustling leaves serve as a backdrop to your explorations.

Winter: Warmth and Festive Charm

From December to February, the Cotswolds exude a sense of comfort and enchantment. Villages are decked out in glittering lights, and the festive spirit fills the air with joy. While the cold weather tempts you to bundle up, the charm of Christmas markets, carol music, and seasonal decorations provide a one-of-a-kind experience. Warmth and friendliness are created by roaring fireplaces in quaint pubs, making it a great time for hearty meals and classic afternoon teas.

The Most Appropriate Time for You

The "best" time to visit the Cotswolds is ultimately determined by your personal preferences and the type of experience you seek. Spring will be your inspiration if you are drawn to vivid blooms, energizing walks, and the promise of new beginnings. Summer is the season for languid days in the sun, outdoor activities, and leisurely exploration. Autumn calls if you're drawn by the poetry of changing leaves, peaceful walks through woodlands, and the artistic attraction of autumn hues. Winter greets you if you desire for the intimacy of comfortable winter days, festive charm, and the embrace of holiday rituals.

Local Festivals & Events

Remember that the Cotswolds' allure isn't confined to the seasons; it's also reflected in the region's calendar of events and festivals. There's always something to enhance your experience, from the Cotswold Olimpick Games to Christmas markets and literary festivals. Look for local events that coincide with your vacation dates to add authenticity and fun to your journey.

Finally, every season is a masterpiece.

Every season adds its unique thread to the vast tapestry of the Cotswolds, weaving together a masterpiece of beauty and inspiration. Whatever time of year you choose to visit, your vacation will be defined by the everlasting beauty of the Cotswolds and the experiences that speak to your heart. Each season has its own secrets waiting to be discovered by your keen senses. Whether you're drawn to the promise of spring blossoms, the sun-drenched days of summer, the colorful palette of autumn, or the warm charm of winter, your journey through the Cotswolds is a celebration of life's changing rhythms and nature's enduring beauty.

Recommendations for Stay Duration

The optimal length of your Cotswolds adventure is an important component of planning. In this section, we'll show you how to strike a balance between seeing the attractions and immersing yourself in the region's many offerings. We'll walk you through the options to ensure that your stay matches with your interests and allows you to discover the Cotswolds' riches at your own speed, whether you're planning a quick vacation or an extended investigation.

Weekend Getaway: Experience Village Life

If you only have a weekend, a weekend getaway provides a tantalizing insight into the Cotswolds' beauty. When you arrive on Friday evening, you'll enjoy a delicious dinner at a local bar or restaurant, immersing yourself in the area's warm friendliness. Saturday unveils the heart of village life—visit a charming village, such as Bourton-on-the-Water with its tranquil streams or Broadway with its panoramic vistas. Take a leisurely stroll through antique shops, explore historic sites, and have a leisurely lunch. Before you leave, take a walk in the countryside or visit a local market on Sunday. While your time is limited, it leaves you wanting more.

Extended Weekend: Expanding Your Knowledge

A three- to four-day weekend stay provides a more immersive experience. You'll have more time to see communities and learn about their histories if you arrive on a Thursday. Consider attending guided tours that provide insights into the Cotswolds' design and stories. Consider taking a short trek along the Cotswold Way National Trail to take in the scenery. With an extra day, you may also participate in courses, such as traditional crafts or cooking classes, to immerse yourself in the cultural past of the Cotswolds.

Week of Exploration: Discovering Hidden Treasures

A week-long excursion reveals the hidden beauties of the Cotswolds and provides a well-rounded experience. You'll have plenty of time to explore the Cotswold Way National Trail, stopping at points that speak to you. Explore the Cotswolds' market towns, each with its own personality and appeal. Consider spending a day seeing historical sites like Sudeley Castle or the old Rollright Stones. This time allows you to participate in community events, see local theatrical shows, and thoroughly absorb the pace of life in the area.

More Than a Week: In-Depth Immersion

For those looking for a more in-depth investigation, staying more than a week allows you to truly immerse yourself in the spirit of the Cotswolds. Longer treks along the Cotswold Way will reveal fresh landscapes and views each day. Immerse yourself in the rhythms of village life, possibly by taking part in local activities or volunteering. You'll have the opportunity to explore lesser-known settlements, learning about their distinct stories and hidden treasures. This time frame allows you to create a genuinely tailored and engaging vacation, from photography classes to nature expeditions.

Personalize to Your Needs

Finally, the length of your stay in the Cotswolds should suit your interests and tastes. Whether you're a fan of architecture, wildlife, history, or simply want to unwind, customize your agenda to meet your needs. The beauty of the Cotswolds is that it can be appreciated in both rapid bursts and leisurely meandering, with each length providing a unique perspective and a plethora of activities.

Take Advantage of the Opportunities

No matter how long you stay, remember that every minute in the Cotswolds is an opportunity to make lasting memories. Every encounter, whether sipping tea in a tearoom, visiting centuries-old alleyways, or staring out over stunning vistas, contributes to the fabric of your voyage. So, whether you're planning a weekend getaway or a longer trip, embrace the opportunity to thoroughly immerse yourself in the wonders of the Cotswolds.

2.3 Choosing a Place to Stay

Welcome to the "Choosing Accommodation Options" section, where you'll find a wide range of lodging options that promise to improve your Cotswolds experience. This section will help you find the perfect home away from home, from charming village inns to opulent rural estates. We'll explore the Cotswolds' broad choice of hotels, ensuring that your stay is not just pleasant but also symbolic of the region's distinct character. Let's have a look at the options available to you, each boasting its own unique blend of comfort, charm, and Cotswolds hospitality.

2.3.1 Inns and Hotels

Hotels and inns in the Cotswolds provide a beautiful blend of luxury, convenience, and local charm. Whether you're looking for a cozy inn in a charming village or a magnificent hotel with modern amenities, the Cotswolds have a wide range of options to suit every traveler's needs. Here, we'll present you to several great options that guarantee proximity to sights and transportation, ensuring that your stay is not only enjoyable but also enriched by the appeal of the Cotswolds.

1. Broadway's Lygon Arms

The Lygon Arms, located in the charming village of Broadway, is a historic hotel that exudes timeless beauty. This hotel, which dates back to the 16th century, combines legacy with modern elegance. Because of its prominent location, it is convenient to Broadway's boutique shops, art galleries, and the famed Broadway Tower. The Lygon Arms has charming suites, superb cuisine, and a spa where you may unwind after a long day of travel.

2. Bibury's Swan Inn

The Swan Inn, located in the historic town of Bibury, embodies Cotswold charm. This inn, which overlooks the River Coln and Arlington Row, offers modest rooms with a hint of rustic luxury. Wake up to peaceful vistas and a full Cotswold breakfast before setting out on your activities. The inn's proximity to Bibury's attractions makes it a great starting point for exploring the village's historic sites.

3. Tetbury's The Close Hotel

The Close Hotel in Tetbury is a hidden gem for anyone looking for a mix of luxury and tranquillity. This Georgian estate has been converted into a boutique hotel with beautiful rooms, lovely grounds, and a Michelin-starred restaurant. The Close Hotel is conveniently located near attractions such as Tetbury Market House and Highgrove House, the Prince of Wales' house.

4. Stroud's Bear of Rodborough

The Bear of Rodborough, perched on a hill with sweeping views of the Cotswolds, is a classic inn with a pleasant and welcoming environment. This inn is a short drive from Stroud and close to attractions such as Woodchester Mansion and Westonbirt Arboretum. Explore the surrounding countryside while eating hearty meals at the inn's restaurant.

5. Cheltenham's Greenway Hotel and Spa

The Greenway Hotel and Spa in Cheltenham is a sophisticated choice for a sumptuous escape. This country house hotel provides nicely designed rooms, a spa for relaxation, and award-winning restaurants. The attractions of Cheltenham, including the famed Cheltenham Racecourse, are easily accessible.

Considerations for Cost

The cost of lodging in the Cotswolds varies depending on criteria such as the type of room, location, and amenities provided. Mid-range hotels and inns typically cost between £100 and £200 per night, while luxury options start at £250 and go up from there. Keep in mind that costs can vary depending on season and availability, so it's best to book ahead of time, especially if you plan to visit during high season.

Booking Suggestions

Consider the features that are most important to you, the closeness to attractions, and transit alternatives when reserving your hotel or inn. Many places have online booking, which allows you to browse hotel options, read guest reviews, and make secure reservations ahead of time. Furthermore, if you intend to utilize public transportation, make sure that your lodging is conveniently located near bus stops or railway stations to make your tour as easy as possible.

Your Cotswolds Retreat is waiting for you.

Whether you stay in a historic inn, a boutique hotel, or an opulent manor, your lodging in the Cotswolds is more than simply a place to sleep—it's an experience in and of itself. As you settle into your chosen residence, you'll find yourself engulfed in the embrace of the Cotswolds, ready to explore the cities, landscapes, and adventures that lie just outside your doorstep.

2.3.2 Hotels with Bed and Breakfast

Bed and breakfasts (B&Bs) in the Cotswolds provide a warm embrace of hospitality and a genuine relationship to the local way of life for guests seeking a more intimate and customized experience. In this section, we'll introduce you to the world of bed and breakfasts, where pleasant lodgings and delicious meals are complemented by your hosts' kindness. B&Bs, which range from lovely cottages to historic houses, allow you to immerse yourself in the spirit of the Cotswolds while enjoying the amenities of a home away from home.

1. Honeysuckle Cottage Bed and Breakfast, Bourton-on-the-Water

Honeysuckle Cottage B&B, located in the heart of Bourton-on-the-Water, provides a relaxing retreat. This cottage has Cotswold beauty with its thatched roof and beautiful gardens. The hosts provide customized care and local knowledge to make your stay unforgettable. Discover the wonders of the hamlet, such as the Model hamlet and Birdland Park, which are only a short walk away.

2. Cirencester's Old Brewhouse

The Old Brewhouse in Cirencester is a bed & breakfast with a rich history that combines luxury and comfort. The rooms include period elements, and the central location makes it simple to visit Cirencester's market town and the Corinium Museum. Enjoy a delicious breakfast and interact with the hosts, who frequently give stories and recommendations.

3. Broadway's Windrush House

Windrush House in Broadway is a welcoming bed and breakfast surrounded by gorgeous gardens. The hosts provide true Cotswold hospitality and are keen to share their enthusiasm for the region. With Broadway's attractions right outside your door, you can visit the Gordon Russell Design Museum or go on countryside walks. The comfortable rooms and personalized attention make for an unforgettable visit.

4. Broadway and Abbots Grange

Try Abbots Grange in Broadway for a taste of historic grandeur. This medieval manor house converted B&B offers luxury accommodations with stunning Cotswolds views. Abbots Grange, England's oldest B&B, transports you back in time while providing modern conveniences. Explore the charms of Broadway while relaxing on the estate's grounds.

5. Stow-on-the-Wold Old Post Office

The Old Post Office B&B, located in the center of Stow-on-the-Wold, combines history with comfort. The rooms are decorated with traditional characteristics, and the hosts greet you with open arms. The market center and ancient sites of Stow-on-the-Wold are a short walk away, allowing you to immerse yourself in the village's ambience.

Personal Relationships and Local Knowledge

One of the distinguishing benefits of staying in a B&B is the opportunity to interact with your hosts. They frequently provide excellent local insights, pointing out hidden jewels and off-the-beaten-path places that aren't commonly known. Engaging in meaningful conversations with hosts and fellow tourists over breakfast can also lead to the exchange of travel experiences.

Considerations for Booking

Consider the type of experience you want when hiring a bed and breakfast. B&Bs provide various amenities, and some may have communal or en-suite bathrooms. As with any accommodation, it's best to book ahead of time, especially during peak seasons. B&Bs may provide a personalized touch, so discuss any specific needs or dietary preferences when making your stay.

Making Long-lasting Memories

Staying in a Cotswolds bed and breakfast is about more than just finding a place to sleep—it's about creating memories and developing connections. Your B&B stay adds a depth of authenticity to your Cotswolds trip, from waking up to the aroma of a freshly prepared breakfast to chatting with hosts who are passionate about showcasing their region.

2.3.3 Self-Contained Cottages

Self-catering cottages provide a unique opportunity to fully immerse oneself in the Cotswolds' environment and lifestyle. We'll dig into the world of self-catering lodgings in this part, where you may enjoy the luxuries of a lovely cottage while having the freedom to establish your own schedule. From quaint thatched roofs to modern facilities, these cottages transform into your private vacation, allowing you to live like a local and explore the Cotswolds at your own speed.

1. Chipping Campden Cotswold Cottage Retreat

This peaceful retreat is located in the lovely market town of Chipping Campden. The Cotswold Cottage Retreat exudes rustic beauty with its exposed timbers and classic features. You can prepare meals using local items in the fully equipped kitchen. Take leisurely strolls along Chipping Campden's historic High Street, connecting with the town's artistic community.

2. Bourton-on-the-Water Artist's Loft

Try The Artist's Loft, a small cottage in Bourton-on-the-Water, for a one-of-a-kind experience. This loft-style housing provides a creative and pleasant environment. Prepare your meals in the well-equipped kitchenette and eat them while looking out over the peaceful village. Being in Bourton-on-the-Water allows you to easily access attractions and riverside walks.

3. Rose Cottage is located in Stow-on-the-Wold.

Rose Cottage in Stow-on-the-Wold is a classic stone cottage that invites you to journey back in time. This cottage, with its well kept features and vintage appeal, provides an insight into Cotswold history. The cottage's kitchen allows you to prepare your own meals, and Stow-on-the-Wold market square is only a short walk away, making it easy to explore and experience local cuisine.

4. Tetbury's Granary

The Granary is a self-catering cottage in the scenic countryside near Tetbury that combines modern amenities with rural tranquillity. The open-plan concept provides a sense of openness and allows you to experiment with local ingredients in the huge kitchen. The location of the home is ideal for experiencing Tetbury's market town and its surrounding attractions.

5. The Burford Windmill

Try The Windmill in Burford for a one-of-a-kind stay in a historic structure converted into a delightful self-catering property. This windmill provides a one-of-a-kind experience with its circular design and panoramic vistas. The fully equipped kitchen allows you to prepare meals while admiring the interior of the windmill. Explore the charming alleys of Burford and take in the vistas of the Windrush Valley.

How to Live Like a Local

Staying in a self-catering home allows you to live like a local, choosing your own schedule and soaking up the Cotswolds' rhythm. Visit local markets to get fresh products and learn about the region's culinary heritage. Take long treks to uncover secret places and meet the people. Whether you're sipping tea by the window or eating a home-cooked meal, your cottage transforms into a refuge of comfort and authenticity.

Considerations for Action

When booking a self-catering cottage, be sure that the size, amenities, and location fit your needs. Many cottages supply necessities for your stay, but it's a good idea to double-check what is provided and what you may need to bring. Inquire about check-in procedures as well as any particular instructions for your stay. Booking ahead of time is advised, especially during peak seasons.

Creating Memorable Experiences

A self-catering cottage is more than simply a place to stay; it's an invitation to create amazing memories. Your cottage stay allows you to fully accept the essence of the Cotswolds and create memories that will last long after your vacation ends, from creating meals with local foods to relaxing by the fireplace or enjoying the peacefulness of the countryside.

2.3.4 Budget-Friendly Alternatives

There are a range of budget-friendly hotel options available for budget-conscious guests looking to experience the beauty and attraction of the Cotswolds without sacrificing quality. In this section, we'll introduce you to cost-effective options that will allow you to enjoy the Cotswolds' character, explore its attractions, and create memorable memories without breaking the bank. From comfortable hostels to low-cost inns, these options demonstrate that you may experience the splendor of the Cotswolds without breaking the bank.

1. Stow-on-the-Wold Youth Hostel, Stow-on-the-Wold

YHA Stow-on-the-Wold is an excellent choice for budget-conscious travelers who don't want to sacrifice comfort. In the centre of Stow-on-the-Wold, this youth hostel provides clean and pleasant accommodation. The communal areas encourage connection with other guests, and the hotel's central location allows you to easily explore Stow-on-the-World's charm, historic buildings, and local cuisine.

2. Moreton-in-Marsh's Bell Inn

The Bell Inn in Moreton-in-Marsh provides affordable lodging without sacrificing Cotswold charm. This old inn has pleasant accommodations and a welcoming atmosphere. Take advantage of the inn's proximity to the Moreton-in-Marsh train station, which will allow you to conveniently access transportation alternatives for your adventures.

3. The Mousetrap Inn is located in Bourton-on-the-Water.

The Mousetrap Inn, located in the picturesque town of Bourton-on-the-Water, offers cheap lodgings and a traditional Cotswold experience. After a day of sightseeing, the modest rooms of the inn give a welcome respite. Explore the village's attractions, such as the Model Village and the Cotswold Motoring Museum, which are both within walking distance.

4. Charlton Kings' Horse and Groom Inn

The Horse and Groom Inn in Charlton Kings provides affordable rooms in a beautiful environment. This inn, located just a short drive from Cheltenham, allows you to visit the town's attractions, including the Cheltenham Racecourse and the Pittville Pump Room. The inn's friendly atmosphere and reasonable costs make it an excellent alternative for budget-conscious guests.

5. Long Compton's Red Lion Inn

The Red Lion Inn, located in the village of Long Compton, provides cheap lodgings with a rustic character. Because of the inn's central location, you can visit neighboring attractions such as the Rollright Stones and the countryside. Enjoy a delicious supper in the inn's kitchen while taking in the atmosphere of the Cotswolds.

Budget-Friendly Suggestions

When looking for low-cost hotels, try vacationing during off-seasons when prices are cheaper. Consider options that offer shared facilities or smaller room designs, as they can typically result in cost savings. Before making your reservation, read the guest reviews and verify on any additional fees or charges.

Immersing Oneself in Cotswolds Magic

Choosing a low-cost hotel does not imply foregoing the Cotswolds' allure. As you tour lovely villages, walk down riverbank roads, and discover hidden corners, you'll realize that the essence of the

Cotswolds is available to all visitors, regardless of budget. Your tour through this timeless region demonstrates how the Cotswolds' true treasures are woven within its landscapes, villages, and the experiences you make.

2.4 Transportation Suggestions

Welcome to the "Transportation Tips" section, where we'll walk you through the many Cotswolds transportation alternatives. This area is your compass for navigating around this wonderful region, from picturesque drives to efficient public transportation. We'll assist you understand the benefits and drawbacks of each mode of transportation, ensuring that your trip through the Cotswolds is not only enjoyable but also stress-free. Whether you plan to drive, ride the train, or rely on local buses, we have knowledge to help you navigate with confidence. Let us embark on a voyage across the transportation network of the Cotswolds to discover the secrets of seamless exploration.

2.4.1 How to Get to the Cotswolds

Your Cotswolds experience begins with traveling to this gorgeous region, and we'll give you a complete guide to getting there in this section. We'll investigate the many transportation options available, ensuring that your travel is as seamless as possible, whether you're arriving from inside the UK or from abroad.

1. Taking the Train

If you're traveling from London, using the train is one of the most convenient methods to get to the Cotswolds. Departing from London Paddington, there are direct train services to Cotswold towns such as Moreton-in-Marsh, Cheltenham, and Stroud. The ride offers stunning vistas of the countryside, providing an excellent introduction to the region's natural beauties.

If you're traveling from another major city, connecting trains can take you to Cotswold attractions. Direct links to many Cotswold towns are also available via routes from Birmingham, Bristol, and Oxford.

2. By Car

Driving from London: If you prefer freedom and the opportunity to explore the region at your own leisure, driving to the Cotswolds from London is an alternative. Depending on your destination, the journey will take between two and three hours. The M40 and A40 are major thoroughfares that provide easy access to places such as Burford, Stow-on-the-Wold, and Chipping Norton.

From Other Cities: Major road networks connect the Cotswolds to other cities, allowing road excursions from other parts of the UK possible. Prepare for some tiny country lanes and utilize GPS or navigation applications to navigate through the villages.

3. By Bus

Coaches: National Express operates coach services from major cities to Cotswold towns. These buses provide travelers a cost-effective option. Check schedules and routes ahead of time, as direct connections to all sites may not be available.

4. By Air

Airports: If you're flying in from another country, local airports such as Birmingham Airport, Bristol Airport, and London Heathrow Airport provide convenient access to the Cotswolds. You can travel to your chosen Cotswold town via train, bus, or auto hire once you arrive.

5. Considerations for Planning

Advance Ticket Purchase: Whether traveling by train or coach, purchasing your tickets in advance can often result in cost savings. Furthermore, during peak tourist seasons, purchasing your tickets early ensures availability.

Cotswold towns such as Moreton-in-Marsh, Cheltenham, and Stroud function as transit hubs, connecting to neighboring towns and villages. You can arrange your arrival and departure based on these locations for convenience.

Local Transportation: Once in the Cotswolds, consider using local transportation options like buses and taxis to explore the area. In rural places, public transportation may be restricted, so plan your routes and schedules accordingly.

Getting to the Cotswolds is the start of an incredible experience. Whether you take the comfort of a train, the freedom of a car, or the cost-effectiveness of a bus, your travel here sets the tone for your exploration of this timeless location. As you travel through stunning landscapes and approach lovely villages, you'll get a sense of impending discovery of the Cotswolds' beauty, history, and enchantment.

2.4.2 Region Wide Public Transportation

Once you've arrived in the Cotswolds, exploring the area is made simple by a variety of public transit options. In this section, we'll go over how to use buses, trains, and other kinds of public transportation to get around the Cotswolds' charming villages, historic attractions, and natural splendor.

1. Buses

Local Bus Services: A network of local bus services connects towns and villages throughout the Cotswolds. Buses are an excellent way to go to locations that may not be accessible by train. Timetables and itineraries are subject to change, so double-check timetables ahead of time.

Consider purchasing explorer tickets, which provide unrestricted travel on buses inside the Cotswolds for a specific period of time. These tickets allow you to explore different locations and attractions without having to acquire individual tickets for each journey.

2. Trains

Cotswold Line: The Cotswold Line is a picturesque train route that connects communities such as Moreton-in-Marsh, Kingham, and Charlbury in the Cotswolds. The train ride offers breathtaking vistas of rolling hills and lovely towns, making the journey itself a delight.

Rail Passes: Rail passes, such as the Cotswold Discovery Pass, can provide unlimited Cotswold Line travel for a set period of time. These passes are an inexpensive option to tour the area by train while taking in the surroundings.

3. Cycling

Cycle Paths & Trails: Cycling is a popular way for outdoor enthusiasts to enjoy the landscape of the Cotswolds. The area has a network of cycle lanes and trails that take you through scenic landscapes and allow you to find hidden jewels at your own speed.

Bike Rentals: There are bike rental shops in many towns and villages where you may borrow a bicycle for the day. Exploring the Cotswolds on two wheels provides a distinct perspective, whether you're a seasoned cyclist or a casual rider.

4. Walking

Local Walks: The Cotswolds has a plethora of walking routes for people of all fitness levels and interests. There is a trail for every style of tourist, from pleasant village strolls to strenuous hikes.

Guided Tours: Take advantage of guided walking tours led by local experts who impart information about the region's history, nature, and culture. These excursions give you a better understanding of the places you visit.

5. Practical Suggestions

Timetables & Schedules: Before embarking on your tour, familiarize yourself with bus and train schedules. Schedules are subject to vary, particularly on weekends and holidays.

Local Information Centers: Visit Cotswold towns' local information centers for maps, schedules, and advice on the best transportation alternatives for accessing specific sights or villages.

Plan Your Routes: To make the most of your stay in the Cotswolds, plan your routes and connections ahead of time. To stay up to date on schedules and directions, consider using transportation applications or websites.

Uninterrupted Exploration

Public transportation in the Cotswolds opens up a whole new realm of discovery, allowing you to go off the beaten road and discover the region's hidden gems. Whether you're taking a bus to a charming village, taking a gorgeous train ride through the countryside, cycling along picturesque paths, or beginning a leisurely walk, each means of transportation guarantees an amazing experience and an intimate connection to the soul of the Cotswolds.

2.4.3 Automobile Rentals and Driving

Car rentals allow you to explore the Cotswolds at your leisure, giving you access to hidden jewels, attractive towns, and scenic roads that public transportation may not provide. In this section, we'll walk you through the car rental procedure, highlight reliable car rental businesses, and provide crucial driving recommendations to guarantee a pleasant and enjoyable trip through the Cotswolds.

1. Renting a Vehicle

Choosing the Right Car: Choose a vehicle that meets your needs and tastes. Consider size, comfort, and luggage space whether you're traveling alone, as a couple, or with a group.

Booking in Advance: It is preferable to book your vehicle hire in advance to assure the greatest rates and availability, especially during peak travel seasons. Online booking platforms allow you to quickly compare prices and options.

2. Reputable Car Rental Firms

Avis is a well-known car rental company with a strong presence in the United Kingdom. They provide a variety of car options as well as convenient pickup locations, including major airports and cities.

Enterprise: Enterprise provides a diverse range of vehicles, including economy cars, SUVs, and others. They have several locations throughout the Cotswolds, making it simple to pick up and return your rental.

Hertz: Hertz is known for its dependability and customer service and has a diverse fleet of vehicles. Their rental site network includes many Cotswold towns and transportation hubs.

3. Driving in the Cotswolds

Driving on the Left: Cars in the United Kingdom drive on the left side of the road. If you're used to driving on the right, give yourself some time to adjust.

Narrow roads: Many of the Cotswold roads are delightfully narrow and winding. Drive carefully, especially in villages, and be prepared for oncoming traffic.

Parking: Most Cotswold towns have public parking lots where you can leave your rented car safely. Parking is also available at some accommodations.

4. Exploring with Liberty

Off-the-Beaten-Path Adventures: Renting a car allows you to visit places that are not easily accessible by public transportation. Explore hidden villages, rolling farmland, and scenic viewpoints.

The Cotswolds is known for its beautiful drives, such as the Cotswold Way and the Romantic Road. You can start on these scenic routes with a rental car and capture stunning vistas along the way.

Local Flavors: Driving allows you to stop at local markets, farm stands, and quaint tea rooms to savor regional cuisine and engage with the culinary culture of the Cotswolds.

5. Driving Manners

Speed Limits: Follow posted speed limits in miles per hour (mph). Speed limits can differ depending on the type of road you're on.

Roundabouts: Roundabouts are common in the United Kingdom. Yield to vehicles already in the roundabout and enter only when it is safe to do so.

Use of Lights: In low visibility conditions, such as rain or fog, use dipped headlights to ensure your vehicle is visible to other drivers.

Renting a car in the Cotswolds opens the door to a world of discovery, giving you the freedom to uncover the region's treasures at your own pace. From quaint villages to rolling hills, every turn of the road shows a new facet of the Cotswolds' beauty. By choosing the right rental company, practicing safe driving etiquette, and embracing the joys of the open road, you're going on a journey that promises discovery, connection, and unforgettable memories.

2.4.4 Cycling Routes and Bike Rentals

For cycling enthusiasts and those eager to experience the Cotswolds from a different viewpoint, cycling routes offer a unique way to immerse yourself in the region's beauty and charm. In this section, we'll guide you through the diverse cycling routes available, provide tips for a safe and enjoyable cycling experience, and introduce you to bike rental options that will equip you for an unforgettable trip on two wheels.

1. Cycling Routes

Cotswold Way: The Cotswold Way is a renowned long-distance trail that spans over 100 miles, offering cyclists the opportunity to traverse picturesque landscapes, historic sites, and charming towns. Choose parts of the trail that match your fitness level and interests.

Family-Friendly Routes: If you're traveling with family, there are gentle, family-friendly routes that are great for leisurely cycling. These paths are often flat and well-suited for riders of all ages.

2. Cycling Safety and Etiquette

Safety Gear: Wearing a helmet is important for your safety. Additionally, consider wearing high-visibility clothing to improve your visibility to other road users.

Follow Traffic Rules: When cycling on roads, stick to traffic rules and signals. Use hand signals to show turns, and follow road signs and markings.

Respect Other Road Users: Share the road with pedestrians and cars. Give pedestrians the right of way, and be careful around vehicles, especially in narrow lanes.

3. Bike Rentals

Local Bike Shops: Many towns and villages in the Cotswolds have bike rental shops that offer a range of bicycles for different terrains and preferences. These shops can provide information on suitable routes and equipment.

Cycle Tour Companies: Consider taking a guided cycling tour, where equipment is often supplied. These tours offer the advantage of local knowledge, group camaraderie, and pre-planned routes.

4. Exploring by Bike

Picturesque Landscapes: Cycling allows you to take in the Cotswolds' stunning landscapes at a leisurely pace. Pedal through rolling hills, fields, and alongside charming rivers.

Village Exploration: Use your bike to explore quaint Cotswold towns, where you can stop for a cup of tea, browse local shops, and capture the essence of village life.

5. Practical Suggestions

Route Planning: Before setting out, plan your cycling route and ensure it fits your skill level and interests. Consider elevation changes, landscape, and distance.

Pack Essentials: Carry essentials such as water, snacks, a map, and a cell phone. Be prepared for changing weather conditions, and pack clothes accordingly.

Cycling Etiquette: Be courteous to walkers, other cyclists, and drivers. Signal your intentions clearly, and pass others safely, giving ample space.

Pedal into Cotswold Beauty

Cycling routes in the Cotswolds offer a captivating and eco-friendly way to explore the region's wonders. As you pedal through charming villages, breathe in the fresh countryside air, and enjoy the feeling of freedom that cycling brings, you'll connect with the Cotswolds on an intimate level. By adhering to safety guidelines, embracing the joy of exploration, and picking a path that resonates with you, your cycling adventure promises to be a memory-rich journey through the Cotswold splendor.

Top Attractions in the Cotswolds

Welcome to the "Top Attractions in the Cotswolds" chapter, where we'll take you on a captivating trip through the region's most iconic and enchanting destinations. From historic landmarks to natural wonders, charming villages to cultural hotspots, this area is your guide to finding the Cotswolds' must-visit places. Immerse yourself in centuries of history, soak in breathtaking scenery, and unravel the Cotswolds' allure as we reveal the treasures that await your exploration. Let's start on a tour of the Cotswolds' top attractions, each one promising a unique and unforgettable experience.

3.1 Historic Villages and Towns

3.1.1 Bourton-on-the-Water

Welcome to Bourton-on-the-Water, a quintessential Cotswold town that captures the essence of the region's charm and beauty. As you step into this picturesque haven, you'll be greeted by the soothing melody of the River Windrush gently flowing through the heart of the town. Bourton-on-the-Water is a destination that encapsulates the Cotswolds' historic character, rich history, and tranquil ambiance. Let's start on a journey through the village's cobblestone streets, uncovering its treasures and timeless allure.

1. A Riverside Gem

Bourton-on-the-Water is often referred to as the "Venice of the Cotswolds" due to its number of elegant low bridges that span across the River Windrush. These charming stone bridges create a unique atmosphere, inviting you to take leisurely strolls along the water's edge and savor the reflections of the village's historic buildings reflected in the gentle ripples.

2. Model Village

Immerse yourself in the village's unique sights, starting with the Model Village. This one-ninth scale replica of Bourton-on-the-Water itself is an amazing feat of craftsmanship. Marvel at the intricate detail of the miniature town, complete with miniature trees, houses, and even the replica of the replica, known as the "Doomsday Model."

3. Birdland Park and Gardens

For nature lovers, Birdland Park and Gardens offer a delightful escape. Explore unusual birds from around the world, including penguins, flamingos, and parrots. Wander through tranquil gardens and meet interesting species while learning about their habitats and conservation efforts.

4. Cotswold Motoring Museum

Step back in time at the Cotswold driving Museum, where vintage cars and nostalgic exhibits transport you to the early days of driving. Explore the evolution of automobiles and discover the stories of their owners through a diverse collection of vehicles and memorabilia.

5. Riverside Dining

Indulge in the village's culinary offers with riverside dining experiences that provide panoramic views of the water and surrounding beauty. Whether you're having a traditional cream tea or savoring locally sourced dishes, the village's cafes and restaurants offer a range of options to satisfy your taste buds.

6. Boutique Shopping

Bourton-on-the-Water's charming streets are lined with boutique shops that beckon you to discover their treasures. From handcrafted crafts to unique souvenirs, you'll find an array of items that capture the Cotswolds' character and craftsmanship.

7. Countryside Walks

Surrounded by lush greenery and rolling hills, Bourton-on-the-Water is an ideal starting point for outdoor walks. Follow scenic trails that lead you through the countryside, offering breathtaking vistas and the chance to immerse yourself in the Cotswolds' natural beauty.

8. Practical Suggestions

Getting There: Bourton-on-the-Water is easily available by car and public transportation. Consider using the village's car parks, as parking can be limited due to its fame.

Timing Your Visit: Bourton-on-the-Water is a year-round destination, each season giving its unique charm. Summer brings vibrant gardens, while fall paints the trees in warm hues.

Exploration in Comfort: Wear comfortable footwear as you discover the village's cobblestone streets and attractions. Consider bringing a light jacket, as weather can change suddenly.

Capturing Memories: Don't forget your camera to catch the village's postcard-perfect scenes and moments that will become cherished memories of your Cotswold adventure.

Timeless Beauty

Bourton-on-the-Water is more than a town; it's a journey through time, a connection to nature, and an immersion in the Cotswolds' enchanting spirit. From the tranquility of the river to the allure of historic sites, every corner of Bourton-on-the-Water tells a story and asks you to become a part of its narrative. As you explore its streets, cross its charming bridges, and soak in the atmosphere, you'll experience the Cotswolds' timeless beauty and understand why this village holds a special place in the hearts of those who visit.

3.1.2 Stow-on-the-Wold

Welcome to Stow-on-the-Wold, a captivating Cotswold town that stands as a testament to centuries of history, building, and culture. Nestled atop a hill, Stow-on-the-Wold exudes a timeless charm that draws tourists from far and wide. As you wander through its ancient streets and historic market square, you'll be transported to a bygone era where tradition and technology seamlessly coexist. Join us on a trip through the town's cobblestone lanes, uncovering its treasures and experiencing the allure of Stow-on-the-Wold firsthand.

1. Historic Market Square

Stow-on-the-Wold market place serves as the heart of the town, a hub of activity and history. Flanked by centuries-old buildings, the square has been a gathering place for locals and tourists alike for generations. Enjoy the open-air market held here on select days, where you can peruse stalls offering everything from artisanal crafts to fresh fruit.

2. St. Edward's Church

Dominating the town's skyline is St. Edward's Church, a magnificent structure that speaks to Stow-on-the-Wold's deep-rooted past. Step inside this serene sanctuary and enjoy its exquisite stained glass windows, intricate stonework, and a unique wooden door known as the "door to nowhere."

3. Antique Shops and Galleries

Stow-on-the-World's charming streets are lined with antique shops and galleries that beckon collectors and art lovers. Discover rare finds, vintage treasures, and contemporary art pieces that show the town's artistic spirit and appreciation for craftsmanship.

4. The Old Stocks Inn

Indulge in a dose of luxury and comfort at The Old Stocks Inn, a historic hotel that seamlessly blends traditional building with modern amenities. Whether you're having a sumptuous meal in the restaurant or unwinding in a cozy room, this inn offers an inviting retreat in the heart of Stow-on-the-Wold.

5. Exploring the Countryside

Surrounded by the Cotswolds' lush scenery, Stow-on-the-Wold is an ideal starting point for scenic walks and explorations. Follow footpaths that lead you through rolling hills, charming towns, and idyllic landscapes that define the region's natural beauty.

6. Artisanal Delights

Treat your taste buds to artisanal treats offered by local bakeries, cafes, and eateries. From freshly baked pastries to traditional Cotswold dishes, the town's culinary scene shows its commitment to quality and authenticity.

7. Guided Tours

Enhance your visit by taking guided tours that provide insights into Stow-on-the-Wold's history, architecture, and local stories. Expert guides will lead you through hidden corners, sharing stories that bring the town's past to life.

8. Practical Suggestions

Getting There: Stow-on-the-Wold can be reached by car or public transportation. If coming by car, consider using nearby car parks, as the town's historic center may have limited parking.

Local Events: Check for local events, festivals, and markets that may coincide with your stay. These events offer a glimpse into the town's vibrant group spirit.

Historic Exploration: Wear comfortable shoes suitable for walking on cobblestone streets and visiting historical sites. A camera is a must to record the town's captivating architecture and atmosphere.

Immersing in Heritage: Allow yourself to be transported back in time as you wander through Stow-on-the-Wold's streets, imagining the stories of those who have walked the same paths for ages.

Timeless Elegance

Stow-on-the-Wold stands as a living testament to the Cotswolds' history and legacy. Its historic buildings, vibrant culture, and welcoming atmosphere invite you to step into a world where the past seamlessly meets the present. Whether you're drawn to its market square, captivated by its churches, or inspired by its artistic offerings, Stow-on-the-Wold is a journey that resonates with the soul and captures the heart of every traveler who crosses its doorway.

3.1.3 Bibury

Welcome to Bibury, a fairytale town that seems to have been plucked from the pages of a storybook and brought to life. Nestled along the banks of the River Coln, Bibury enchants tourists with its idyllic charm, picturesque cottages, and timeless tranquility. As you walk through its winding streets and bask in the beauty of its natural surroundings, you'll find yourself immersed in a world where time stands still and the Cotswolds' allure is at its most captivating. Join us on a trip through Bibury's cobblestone lanes and discover the treasures that make it a truly enchanting destination.

1. Arlington Row

A Quintessential Cotswold Scene Prepare to be captivated by Arlington Row, one of the most photographed spots in the Cotswolds. This row of charming cottages, going back to the 17th century, showcases the quintessential Cotswold architecture characterized by honey-hued stone, steep gables, and picturesque gardens.

2. Bibury Trout Farm

For a unique experience, visit the Bibury Trout Farm, one of the oldest in England. Explore the farm's crystal-clear waters, learn about trout raising, and even try your hand at fishing. You can also enjoy a delicious meal featuring fresh trout at the farm's on-site diner.

3. St. Mary's Church

St. Mary's Church stands as a testament to Bibury's historical and spiritual importance. Admire the church's architecture, including its Saxon tower, and step inside to discover beautifully kept medieval windows and intricate woodwork.

4. Bibury Court Gardens

Experience peace in Bibury Court Gardens, where meticulously landscaped gardens, soothing water features, and vibrant flora create a haven of quiet. Take a leisurely stroll through the gardens and find quiet spots to think and rejuvenate.

5. The Swan Hotel

Indulge in luxury and charm at The Swan Hotel, a historic establishment that blends elegant accommodations with modern comforts. Whether you're dining in the restaurant or unwinding in the cozy lounges, The Swan offers a warm and inviting setting.

6. Walking Trails

Explore Bibury's natural beauty by going on scenic walking trails that lead you through the surrounding countryside. Enjoy the sight of wildflowers, fields, and the peaceful River Coln as you immerse yourself in the Cotswolds' landscapes.

7. Traditional Crafts

Bibury's handmade spirit comes to life through traditional crafts. Discover workshops and offices where local craftsmen create pottery, textiles, and other handmade treasures that reflect the village's character and creativity.

8. Practical Suggestions

Accessing Bibury: Bibury is easily accessible by car or public means. If you're driving, parking is available in marked areas near the village center.

Opening Hours: Check the opening hours of attractions and shops, as they may vary based on the season. Some sites may have limited hours during the off-peak months.

Comfortable Attire: Wear comfortable walking shoes ideal for exploring the village's cobblestone streets and nearby trails. A light jacket or layers are recommended, as weather conditions can change.

Photography Opportunities: Don't forget to bring your camera to catch the enchanting scenes and timeless beauty that make Bibury a photographer's dream.

Whispers of Enchantment

Bibury is more than a town; it's a tapestry woven with history, nature, and the Cotswolds' undeniable allure. Each corner reveals a new facet of its enchanting charm, inviting you to pause, reflect, and enjoy the simple joys of life. From the fairytale cottages of Arlington Row to the serenity of its gardens, Bibury whispers stories of centuries past and asks you to become a part of its enduring narrative.

3.1.4 Broadway

Welcome to Broadway, a village that exudes elegance, charm, and the timeless beauty that marks the Cotswolds. Nestled at the foot of the Worcestershire hills, Broadway is a place where history, art, and natural splendor combine to create a truly enchanting destination. As you stroll along its vibrant streets, adorned with golden-hued stone buildings and lush gardens, you'll discover a town that captures the essence of the Cotswolds' allure. Join us on a journey through Broadway's captivating lanes and discover the treasures that make it a jewel within the Cotswold crown.

1. Picturesque High Street

Broadway's High Street is a picture of beauty, lined with traditional Cotswold stone buildings that house a delightful array of shops, boutiques, galleries, and cafes. Stroll along this charming thoroughfare, where each storefront tells a story and invites you to explore its wonders.

2. Broadway Tower

Standing as an iconic symbol, Broadway Tower offers panoramic views that stretch over the Cotswolds and beyond. Climb to the top of this historic tower, built by renowned architect James Wyatt, and witness breathtaking views that capture the region's sprawling landscapes.

3. Historical Significance

Broadway's past is woven into its architecture and character. Discover buildings that date back centuries, such as the old Market Hall, which once served as a shelter for merchants and traders. Let the village's streets transport you to times gone by.

4. Gordon Russell Design Museum

Immerse yourself in art and skill at the Gordon Russell Design Museum. Learn about the legacy of renowned furniture designer Gordon Russell and explore exhibits that feature his innovative designs and contributions to the arts and crafts movement.

5. Cotswold Lavender

Experience the bright beauty and fragrant aroma of Cotswold Lavender. Wander through rows of lavender in full bloom, delighting in the sensory experience and getting postcard-perfect photos of the vivid purple fields.

6. Exploring the Countryside

Broadway is surrounded by captivating countryside that beckons adventure. Lace up your walking shoes and start on trails that wind through meadows, woodlands, and hills, giving a chance to connect with nature.

7. The Lygon Arms

Indulge in luxury at The Lygon Arms, a historic hotel that mixes period features with modern comforts. Dine in elegance at the hotel's restaurants, unwind in cozy lounges, and experience the charm of a bygone age.

8. Practical Suggestions

Reaching Broadway: Broadway can be reached by car or public means. If you're driving, consider using nearby parking spaces, as on-street parking may be limited.

Seasonal Delights: Plan your stay to coincide with the seasons. Spring and summer bring vibrant blooms, while fall paints the landscape in warm hues.

Comfortable Attire: Wear comfortable footwear suited for walking on cobbled streets and exploring trails. Dress in layers to react to changing weather conditions.

Local Cuisine: Savor the flavors of Broadway by dining at its cafes and restaurants, where you can indulge in traditional Cotswold dishes and locally found ingredients.

Elegance in Every Corner

Broadway is more than a town; it's a symphony of elegance, history, and natural beauty that resonates in every corner. From the stunning views atop Broadway Tower to the allure of its artisanal shops, each facet of this village tells a story that intertwines with the Cotswolds' history. As you immerse yourself in its charm, Broadway welcomes you to experience the Cotswolds' finest qualities: timeless elegance, a connection to nature, and an embrace of history.

3.1.5 Moreton-in-Marsh

Welcome to Moreton-in-Marsh, a gateway to the Cotswolds that beckons travelers with its historic charm, lively markets, and cultural wealth. Situated at the crossroads of ancient trading routes, Moreton-in-Marsh boasts a unique character that shows its heritage and vibrancy. As you explore its streets, immerse yourself in its bustling market square, and find its hidden gems, you'll experience a destination that captures the essence of the Cotswolds' allure. Join us on a trip through Moreton-in-Marsh captivating lanes and discover the treasures that make it a truly special Cotswold town.

1. Bustling Market Town

Moreton-in-Marsh's historic market place is a hub of activity and a reflection of the town's vibrant spirit. On market days, the square comes alive with stalls selling everything from fresh produce and artisanal crafts to antiques and unique finds.

2. Stowford Press Visitor Centre

Delve into the world of cider-making at the Stowford Press Visitor Centre. Learn about the cider-making process, its past, and the craftsmanship that goes into producing this iconic beverage. Enjoy tastings and gain insight into a beloved Cotswold ritual.

3. Historic Architecture

The town's architecture is a testament to its rich past. Admire buildings that date back centuries, such as The Redesdale Hall, which serves as both a place for events and a glimpse into Moreton-in-Marsh's past.

4. The Moreton Gallery

Immerse yourself in the local arts scene at The Moreton Gallery. Discover a curated collection of contemporary art, including paintings, sculptures, and ceramics made by local and regional artists.

5. Batsford Arboretum and Garden Centre

Experience the beauty of nature at Batsford Arboretum and Garden Centre. Wander through this expansive arboretum, which displays a diverse collection of trees and plants from around the world. Explore themed gardens, take in the seasonal colors, and enjoy the calm of this botanical haven.

6. Exploring the Countryside

Moreton-in-Marsh is surrounded by the Cotswolds' beautiful countryside. Embark on countryside walks that lead you through rolling hills, charming towns, and scenic landscapes that define the region's natural beauty.

7. The Manor House Hotel

Indulge in luxury and class at The Manor House Hotel. This historic place offers elegant accommodations, fine dining, and a refined atmosphere that invites you to unwind and savor the Cotswolds' best.

8. Practical Suggestions

Accessing Moreton-in-Marsh: Moreton-in-Marsh can be reached by car or public transportation. If you're driving, consider using designated parking places near the town center.

Market Days: Plan your visit to match with market days, held on certain days of the week. These markets offer a glimpse into the town's bustling atmosphere and provide chances for shopping.

Comfortable Attire: Wear comfortable walking shoes ideal for exploring the town's streets and surrounding trails. Dress in layers to react to changing weather conditions.

Local Cuisine: Indulge in local flavors by eating at Moreton-in-Marsh eateries, cafes, and pubs. Sample traditional Cotswold dishes and enjoy the ingredients sourced from the area.

Heritage and Hospitality

Moreton-in-Marsh is more than a town; it's a blend of history, hospitality, and the Cotswolds' enduring charm. From the bustling market square to the serenity of its countryside, each aspect of Moreton-in-Marsh invites you to connect with its rich past and vibrant culture. As you explore its streets and connect with its local community, you'll discover a town that welcomes you with open arms and invites you to become a part of its story.

3.2 Stately Homes and Castles

3.2.1 Blenheim Palace

Welcome to Blenheim Palace, a masterpiece of grandeur, history, and architectural excellence set within the Oxfordshire countryside. This splendid stately home stands as a testament to artistic vision, political legacy, and the enduring spirit of the Churchill family. As you step onto its sprawling grounds and discover its opulent interiors, you'll be transported through time, unraveling layers of history, culture, and arts. Join us on an immersive trip through the halls of Blenheim Palace, where each room tells a story and each vista offers a glimpse into the past.

1. Historical Significance

Blenheim Palace was built as a tribute to John Churchill, the 1st Duke of Marlborough, following his victory over the French at the Battle of Blenheim in 1704. The palace's building was a gesture of gratitude from the country, and its design was entrusted to the esteemed architect Sir John Vanbrugh.

2. Architectural Marvel

The palace's architecture is a marvel of Baroque and English styles, having a symmetrical façade, grand columns, ornate detailing, and sculptural elements that exude elegance and power. Vanbrugh's visionary design seamlessly integrates the palace with the nearby landscape, creating a harmonious blend of nature and architecture.

3. State Rooms and Art Collections

Step inside Blenheim Palace to explore its sumptuous State Rooms, each adorned with opulent furnishings, fine art, and elaborate tapestries. The Long Library, in particular, stands as a breathtaking showcase of literature and art, housing over 10,000 volumes and a stunning painted roof.

4. The Churchill Connection

Blenheim Palace holds special importance as the birthplace of Sir Winston Churchill, one of the 20th century's most iconic leaders. Visit the room where he was born and learn about his remarkable life through exhibitions and displays that chronicle his successes and legacy.

5. Formal Gardens and Grounds

The palace's gardens are a work of horticultural artistry, featuring carefully planned parterres, serene water features, and sweeping lawns. Explore the Water Terraces, the Secret Garden, and the Rose Garden, each giving a unique sensory experience and a feast for the eyes.

6. Parkland and Landscapes

Blenheim Palace's parkland is a masterpiece in its own right, stretching over 2,000 acres. The "Capability" Brown-designed landscape boasts serene lakes, rolling hills, ancient woods, and meandering trails that invite you to immerse yourself in the natural beauty that inspired generations.

7. Themed Exhibitions

Throughout the year, Blenheim Palace hosts captivating themed exhibitions that provide insights into the palace's past, its inhabitants, and the eras it has experienced. These exhibitions offer a better understanding of the social, cultural, and political dynamics that have shaped the palace's narrative.

8. Practical Suggestions

Getting There: Blenheim Palace is available by car or public transportation. On-site parking is provided, and guided transportation options are often offered.

Visiting Hours: Check the palace's official website for the latest information on opening hours, special events, and guided walks.

Guided Tours: Consider joining a guided tour to fully enjoy the palace's history, architecture, and stories. Knowledgeable guides offer insights that improve your experience.

Photography and Souvenirs: Capture the palace's beauty through photography and explore the gift shops for souvenirs that reflect its history and artistry.

Where Time and Artistry Converge

Blenheim Palace is not just a monument; it's a living testament to human achievement, creativity, and historical importance. From its regal architecture to its exquisite art collections, from its lush gardens to its storied halls, each aspect of the palace invites you to step into the pages of history and immerse yourself in a world where time and artistry merge. As you explore its interiors and roam its landscapes, you'll learn that Blenheim Palace is not only a destination but a journey through the rich tapestry of British heritage.

3.2.2 Sudeley Castle

Welcome to Sudeley Castle, a historic treasure set in the heart of the Cotswolds. With a past spanning over a thousand years, Sudeley Castle is a living testament to the ebb and flow of time, royalty, and romantic intrigue. As you step onto its grounds and discover its exquisite interiors, you'll be transported through history, uncovering stories of queens, nobles, and the enduring spirit of this captivating castle. Join us on a trip through the halls of Sudeley

Castle, where each room holds a secret and every corner is adorned with tales of centuries gone by.

1. Royal Connections

Sudeley Castle has been intertwined with royal history since its beginning. It was once the residence of Katherine Parr, the sixth wife of King Henry VIII and the only queen to be buried on private land. Discover the chambers where Katherine lived and find a unique link to Tudor royalty.

2. Architectural Splendor

The castle's architecture is a blend of styles, showcasing the evolution of design over the ages. From the medieval banqueting hall to the Tudor-era additions and Victorian restorations, each architectural feature tells a story of the castle's transformation through time.

3. Katherine Parr's Garden

Explore the enchanting gardens that surround Sudeley Castle, including the romantic garden built in honor of Katherine Parr. Wander through rose-filled pathways, discover secret alcoves, and marvel at the intricate design that pays homage to the queen's legacy.

4. St. Mary's Church

Within the castle grounds lies St. Mary's Church, an ancient place of worship with a rich past. Visit the church to see the tombs of past residents, including Katherine Parr, and experience the tranquility of a place that has witnessed centuries of devotion and remembrance.

5. The Castle's Collections

Step inside the castle's opulent interiors to admire its diverse collection of art, antiques, and historical items. From portraits and tapestries to furniture and rare manuscripts, each piece gives insights into the lives of those who once called Sudeley Castle home.

6. Gardens of Delight

Sudeley Castle's grounds are a masterpiece of horticultural artistry. Immerse yourself in the beauty of the Queen's Garden, the Knot Garden, and the White Garden, each giving a sensory experience that transports you to another time.

7. Guided Tours and Events

Enhance your visit by taking guided tours that offer in-depth insights into the castle's history, architecture, and tales of its inhabitants. Throughout the year, Sudeley Castle hosts events that bring its past to life, from medieval reenactments to cultural festivals.

8. Practical Suggestions

Accessing Sudeley Castle: Sudeley Castle is available by car or public transportation. The castle offers on-site parking for visitors, and guided transportation options are often available.

Operating Hours: Check the official website for the latest information on opening hours, guided trips, and special events.

Comfortable Attire: Wear comfortable walking shoes ideal for exploring the castle's grounds and its various terrains. Dress in layers to handle changing weather conditions.

Items and Refreshments: Explore the castle's gift shop for unique items that capture its history and charm. Refreshments are available on-site, allowing you to rest and savor the castle's ambiance.

A Journey Through Time

Sudeley Castle is not merely a castle; it's a portal to the past, a view into the lives of royalty, and a testament to enduring love and legacy. As you wander through its chambers, look upon its artworks, and immerse yourself in its gardens, you'll feel the echoes of history come alive. Sudeley Castle asks you to step beyond its gates and start on a journey through time, where the threads of royalty, romance, and the Cotswolds' spirit weave a tapestry of enchantment.

3.2.3 Berkeley Castle

Welcome to Berkeley Castle, a timeless bastion of history, intrigue, and aristocratic tradition nestled within the Cotswolds. With a lineage going back over 900 years, Berkeley Castle stands as a living witness to the triumphs, tragedies, and tales of generations past. As you step into its medieval halls and explore its captivating grounds, you'll be transported through a rich tapestry of history, discovering stories of kings, rebels, and the enduring spirit of this remarkable castle. Join us on a trip through the storied halls of Berkeley Castle, where each stone holds a secret and every corner echoes with the echoes of the past.

1. Medieval Splendor

Berkeley Castle's medieval architecture is a testament to its historical importance. Its imposing stone walls, turrets, and battlements create a sense of medieval grandeur, transporting tourists to an era of knights, feasts, and chivalry.

2. Edward II's Imprisonment

The castle earned notoriety as the site of the imprisonment and brutal murder of King Edward II in 1327. Explore the chamber where Edward II was incarcerated and hear the haunting echoes of a sad chapter in English history.

3. The Berkeley Family

For ages, the Berkeley family has been intricately linked with the castle's history. Discover the family's lineage, tales of their impact, and the legacies they've left behind that continue to shape the castle's identity.

4. Living History

Berkeley Castle offers immersive experiences that allow tourists to step back in time. Encounter costumed characters who bring the past to life, engaging you with stories, demonstrations, and a glimpse into daily life during different times.

5. The Castle's Collections

Step inside the castle's chambers to view its impressive collection of art, artifacts, and historical relics. From intricate tapestries to armor and weaponry, each piece offers a view into the past and the lives of those who inhabited the castle.

6. Gardens and Grounds

Berkeley Castle's parks and grounds offer a serene escape from the modern world. Explore the tranquil surroundings, wander through manicured gardens, and appreciate the breathtaking views of the nearby farmland.

7. Guided Tours and Events

Enhance your visit by taking guided tours that provide insights into the castle's history, architecture, and stories of its inhabitants. Throughout the year, Berkeley Castle hosts events that celebrate its history, from medieval reenactments to seasonal festivals.

8. Practical Suggestions

Accessing Berkeley Castle: Berkeley Castle is accessible by car and is situated within the Cotswolds' picturesque landscape. The castle offers designated parking areas for visitors.

Opening Hours and Tours: Check the castle's official website for the latest information on opening hours, guided tours, and special events.

Appropriate Attire: Wear comfortable shoes appropriate for exploring the castle's grounds and historic interiors. Dress in layers to handle changing weather conditions.

Souvenirs and Refreshments: Browse the castle's gift shop for unique souvenirs that capture its history and beauty. Enjoy drinks on-site to savor the castle's ambiance.

Echoes of the Past

Berkeley Castle is more than an architectural marvel; it's a portal to history, a glimpse into lives lived and legends made. As you traverse its halls, marvel at its artistry, and roam its gardens, you'll sense the echoes of past footsteps and the whispers of centuries-old tales. Berkeley Castle invites you to step beyond its gates and start on a journey through time, where the shadows of kings, rebels, and a dynasty's legacy converge in a tapestry of lasting fascination.

3.3 Natural Landscapes

3.3.1 Cotswold Hills and Scenic Walks

Welcome to the Cotswold Hills, a landscape that represents the very essence of the region's charm and allure. These undulating hills, blanketed in emerald green and adorned with picturesque towns, offer a canvas of natural beauty that invites discovery and introspection. As you travel the scenic walks that crisscross this terrain, you'll be transported through time, finding panoramic vistas, hidden valleys, and a tapestry of sights that encapsulate the Cotswolds' spirit. Join us on an immersive trip through the Cotswold Hills and the scenic walks that promise an unforgettable encounter with nature's grandeur.

1. Explore the Cotswold Way

Embark on the Cotswold Way, a long-distance walking trail that runs for 102 miles along the spine of the Cotswold Hills. This iconic trail offers a diverse range of landscapes, from open fields and woodlands to charming towns and historic sites. Walk a segment of the trail to experience its enchantment directly.

2. Broadway Tower and the Beacon

Begin your trip at Broadway Tower, an iconic vantage point that offers sweeping views over the Cotswold landscape. As you climb the tower, the panorama unfolds, showing the patchwork of fields, meadows, and villages that define the region's beauty.

3. Dover's Hill

Venture to Dover's Hill, a natural amphitheater that has played home to centuries of cultural events and festivities. Breathe in the fresh air as you enjoy a leisurely walk along its grassy slopes, taking in the views that have inspired artists and writers.

4. Hidcote Manor Garden

Discover the enchanting Hidcote Manor Garden, a masterpiece of horticultural artistry that shows a number of outdoor "rooms," each with its own unique design and atmosphere. Meander through its intricately planned paths, enjoy vibrant blooms, and find serene spots for contemplation.

5. Rollright Stones

Journey to the Rollright Stones, a prehistoric stone circle surrounded by tales and mystery. Wander among the ancient stones, feel the energy of the landscape, and ponder the stories that have been woven into this sacred place for millennia.

6. Breathtaking Panoramas

As you explore the Cotswold Hills, you'll meet viewpoints that offer breathtaking panoramas. Stop at vantage places like Standish Point, Cleeve Hill, and Uley Bury to watch the majesty of the rolling hills and the villages nestled within.

7. Ancient Woodlands

Immerse yourself in the ancient forests that punctuate the Cotswold Hills. Wander through beech and oak woods, listening to the rustle of leaves underfoot and the symphony of birdsong overhead. Buckholt Wood and Cranham Woods are just a few examples of these natural havens.

8. Practical Suggestions

Footwear and Attire: Wear comfortable hiking boots or sturdy shoes suited for walking on varied terrain. Dress in layers to suit changing weather conditions, and bring a waterproof jacket in case of rain.

Maps and guidance: Carry detailed maps or use guidance apps to guide your way along the walking trails. Be sure to familiarize yourself with the path before setting out.

Respect for Nature: Practice responsible hiking by staying on marked paths, respecting wildlife and plant life, and leaving no trace of your visit. Carry reusable water bottles and snacks to reduce waste.

Safety Precautions: Let someone know your planned route and expected return time. Carry a fully charged phone and a small first aid kit in case of accidents.

A Journey to Remember

The Cotswold Hills and their scenic walks are more than a location; they're a journey through nature's grandeur, history's embrace, and the embrace of a timeless landscape. As you meander through rolling hills, meet ancient stones, and pause at viewpoints that take your breath away, you'll find yourself immersed in a world where each step uncovers new beauty and connection. The Cotswold Hills invite you to become a part of their story, to discover their trails, and to leave with memories etched in your heart.

3.3.2 Cotswold Wildlife and Nature Reserves

Welcome to the Cotswold Wildlife and Nature Reserves, sanctuaries of biodiversity and natural beauty that offer a glimpse into the region's healthy ecosystems. Amidst the picturesque landscapes and charming towns, these areas provide a haven for diverse wildlife, from rare birds to elusive mammals. As you visit these protected areas, you'll become a part of nature's symphony, witnessing the harmony of life and the delicate balance of the natural world. Join us on an immersive trip through the Cotswold Wildlife and Nature Reserves, where each trail, wetland, and woodland is a testament to conservation and the wonders of the wild.

1. Slimbridge Wetland Centre

Embark on a wetland journey at Slimbridge Wetland Centre, where the scenic landscapes come alive with the calls of migrating birds and the rustle of reeds. Discover tranquil lagoons, observation hides, and interactive exhibits that present you to the interesting world of wetland creatures.

2. Westonbirt Arboretum

Experience the wonder of trees at Westonbirt Arboretum, a botanical masterpiece having a collection of over 15,000 trees and shrubs from around the world. Walk along serene pathways, marvel at seasonal displays of color, and learn about the important role of trees in our ecosystem.

3. Greystones Farm Nature Reserve

Explore the unspoiled beauty of Greystones Farm Nature Reserve, where wildflower meadows, ancient woodlands, and various habitats provide a haven for wildlife. Follow walking trails that wind through this serene environment and immerse yourself in the tranquility of nature.

4. Cotswold Water Park

Discover the Cotswold Water Park, a network of over 150 lakes that offer a playground for water-loving wildlife and outdoor lovers. Witness graceful swans, agile dragonflies, and a variety of bird species as they thrive in this unique aquatic environment.

5. Batsford Arboretum

Engage with nature's beauty at Batsford Arboretum, a quiet haven featuring a diverse collection of trees and plants. Wander through its themed gardens, enjoy the changing seasons, and embrace the serenity that comes from connecting with the natural world.

6. Birdwatching Havens

The Cotswolds are a paradise for birdwatchers, with countless species calling these areas home. From elusive kingfishers to majestic birds of prey, keep an eye out for feathered residents and migratory visitors that improve the region's biodiversity.

7. Conservation Efforts

Many of these reserves actively help conservation efforts, protecting endangered species and keeping delicate ecosystems. Learn about the initiatives in place to safeguard wildlife and their habitats, and consider supporting these important endeavors.

8. Practical Suggestions

Respectful Observation: When visiting wildlife reserves, keep a respectful distance from animals and their habitats. Binoculars and cameras with telephoto lenses can help you view wildlife without disturbing them.

Informed Exploration: Research the specific reserves you plan to visit to understand their rules, entry fees, and available amenities. Some reserves offer guided tours and educational events.

Guided Tours and Interpretive Centers: Consider taking guided tours or visiting interpretive centers within the reserves. Knowledgeable guides and engaging exhibits provide insights into the flora, fauna, and conservation efforts.

Appropriate Attire: Wear neutral-colored clothes and sturdy footwear appropriate for walking on varied terrain. Bring bug repellent, sun protection, and a reusable water bottle.

Embracing Nature's Diversity

The Cotswold Wildlife and Nature Reserves are more than protected areas; they're windows into the diversity of life, ecosystems in balance, and the profound beauty of the natural world. As you walk through wetlands, explore arboretums, and watch birds take flight, you'll find yourself immersed in a world where each rustle of leaves and each ripple of water tell a story of interconnectedness. The Cotswold reserves invite you to experience the symphony of nature, to tread lightly, and to leave with a greater appreciation for the delicate balance that supports life.

3.3.3 Exploring Cotswold Water Park

Welcome to Cotswold Water Park, a mosaic of aquatic wonder that spreads across the countryside like a shimmering necklace of lakes. This vast water playground offers a wealth of outdoor activities, serene retreats, and opportunities to connect with nature's watery beauty. As you navigate the waterways, discover secluded coves, and immerse yourself in the park's diverse landscapes, you'll be going on a journey that reveals the many facets of this aquatic paradise. Join us on an immersive exploration of Cotswold Water Park, where each lake, trail, and hideaway offers an unforgettable experience.

1. Lake Activities and Watersports

Cotswold Water Park boasts a plethora of lakes that cater to water lovers of all kinds. Engage in exciting water sports such as sailing, windsurfing, and kayaking on key lakes like Lake 32 and South Cerney Outdoor. Feel the wind in your hair and the spray of water as you revel in the joy of aquatic experiences.

2. Beaches and Relaxation

Discover lakeside beaches that offer a haven for rest and leisure. Spend sun-kissed hours lounging on sandy shores, dipping your toes in the cool waters, and basking in the peace that comes from being immersed in nature's embrace.

3. Birdwatching and Wildlife

The water park is home to a lively array of bird species and wildlife. Lace up your hiking boots and explore the lakeshores and reedbeds, where you can spot beautiful swans, elegant herons, and even elusive kingfishers. Bring your binoculars and enjoy the thrill of birdwatching.

4. Nature Trails and Walking Paths

Immerse yourself in the natural beauty of Cotswold Water Park by walking along beautiful trails that wind through its landscapes. The Core Trail offers a journey through a mosaic of habitats, while the Thames Path provides a riverside stroll that shows the park's diversity.

5. Ashton Keynes and Neigh Bridge Country Parks

Visit Ashton Keynes and Neigh Bridge Country Parks, two havens within Cotswold Water Park. Ashton Keynes boasts tranquil lakeside views, while Neigh Bridge is a retreat where you can relax, fish, and enjoy the surrounding flora and fauna.

6. Canoe Trails and Picnic Spots

Embark on canoe trails that take you through the park's waterways, giving a unique perspective of its beauty. Explore hidden corners, secret inlets, and secluded bays, and enjoy picnics in beautiful spots that invite you to savor the outdoors.

7. Water Park Visitor Centre

Begin your trip at the Cotswold Water Park Visitor Centre, where you can access maps, information, and insights into the park's diverse attractions. Friendly staff can help you plan your trip and ensure you make the most of your visit.

8. Practical Suggestions

Equipment Rentals: Consider renting equipment such as kayaks, canoes, and paddleboards from reliable providers within the water park. Safety tools and briefings are often included.

Weather Preparedness: Check weather forecasts before going out, and bring appropriate clothing and sun protection. Dress in layers to adapt to changing weather.

Conservation and Respect: Practice responsible outdoor ethics by respecting wildlife and adhering to marked paths and water access points. Minimize waste and leave no sign of your visit.

Refreshments and Facilities: Some parts of the water park offer on-site cafes and facilities. Pack a reusable water bottle and snacks, and ask about restroom facilities before setting out.

A Water Wonderland

Cotswold Water Park isn't merely a collection of lakes; it's a water wonderland that beckons you to enjoy the beauty and vitality of the outdoors. Whether you're wanting adrenaline-pumping adventures or serene moments of contemplation, the water park offers a canvas of possibilities. As you glide on the water, listen to the calls of birds, and stroll along tranquil paths, you'll find yourself immersed in a world that reflects the harmony of nature's elements.

3.4 Arts and Culture

3.4.1 Museums and Galleries

Welcome to the Cotswolds, a region where art, history, and culture combine to create a vibrant tapestry of creativity. Amidst the rolling hills and historic villages, you'll discover a wealth of museums and galleries that offer a look into the Cotswolds' artistic soul. As you step into these cultural havens, you'll be transported through time, meeting captivating artworks, intricate crafts, and tales that breathe life into the region's heritage. Join us on an immersive trip through Cotswold's Museums and Galleries, where each exhibit, brushstroke, and sculpture becomes a portal to creativity and inspiration.

1. Holst Birthplace Museum

Delve into the realm of music at the Holst Birthplace Museum, dedicated to the life and work of musician Gustav Holst. Explore the chambers where he spent his formative years, learn about his songs, and immerse yourself in the melodic heritage that echoes through the centuries.

2. Corinium Museum

Step into the Corinium Museum in Cirencester, where history comes life through artefacts that depict the tale of Roman Britain. Discover ancient mosaics, beautiful jewelry, and things that offer insights into the life of folk who once inhabited the Cotswolds.

3. Museum in the Park

Visit the Museum in the Park in Stroud, a cultural gem that celebrates the region's history via art and exhibits. Wander through galleries that explore themes of nature, industry, and creativity, and engage with artworks that embody the Cotswolds' artistic spirit.

4. New Brewery Arts

Experience the artistic heartbeat of the Cotswolds at New Brewery Arts in Cirencester. This modern arts complex offers a varied assortment of exhibitions, workshops, and artist studios. Witness artists at work, admire unusual crafts, and even try your hand at producing your own masterpiece.

5. SIT Select Showcase

Immerse yourself in modern art at the SIT Select Showcase, an annual event that brings together the works of accomplished artists and craftspeople. From pottery to textiles, the exhibition gives a venue for artistic expression that reflects the Cotswolds' modern creative scene.

6. Court Barn Museum

Discover craftsmanship at its best at Court Barn Museum in Chipping Campden. This museum highlights the Arts & Crafts movement and shows objects manufactured by prominent craftspeople. Delve into the principles of this major movement and marvel at the complex creations.

7. Cheltenham Art Gallery and Museum

Journey to the Cheltenham Art Gallery and Museum, where a rich collection awaits. From fine art to decorative arts, the displays provide an insight into the Cotswolds' rich cultural history. Explore paintings, sculptures, and objects that transcend ages.

8. Immersive Workshops and Tours

Many museums and galleries provide intensive workshops, guided tours, and interactive interactions. Consider joining a guided tour to acquire insights into the exhibits, or participate in a workshop to connect with the creative process firsthand.

9. Practical Suggestions

Opening Hours and entry: Check the official websites of museums and galleries for current information on opening hours, entry rates, and any special exhibitions.

Guided Tours & Workshops: Plan your stay by investigating guided tours, workshops, and events given by the museums and galleries. These experiences can provide a deeper understanding of the displays.

Local Artisans & Studios: Consider exploring local artists' studios and galleries, where you can directly connect with makers and obtain unique artworks and crafts.

Photography and Souvenirs: Capture the beauty of artworks and exhibits through photography, following any rules or guidelines offered by the venue. Explore gift shops for gifts that represent the region's creative history.

Artistry Unveiled

Cotswold's Museums and Galleries are more than repositories of objects; they're doorways to creativity, to the tales of bygone times, and to the lively pulse of modern expression. As you browse around exhibit halls, contemplate upon masterpieces, and connect with the tales these artworks tell, you'll become a part of a cultural narrative that has enriched the Cotswolds for decades. The museums and galleries allow you to explore, contemplate, and carry a piece of the Cotswolds' artistic heart with you as you wander across its landscapes.

3.4.2 Performing Arts Venues

Welcome to the Cotswolds, a location that pulses with the harmonies of the performing arts. Amidst the lovely villages and picturesque scenery, you'll discover a tapestry of places where culture comes alive through music, theater, and live performances. As you step into these cultural havens, you'll be taken to the heart of artistic expression, experiencing riveting plays, enchanting concerts, and the enchantment of the stage. Join us on an immersive trip through Cotswolds Performing Arts Venues, where each act, note, and spotlight reflects the region's creative energy.

1. Everyman Theatre, Cheltenham

Experience the thrill of the stage at Everyman Theatre in Cheltenham, a cultural gem that offers a broad assortment of productions. From classic plays to modern performances, immerse yourself in the world of theater as amazing actors bring stories to life.

2. Cheltenham Town Hall

Discover a hub of cultural activities at Cheltenham Town Hall, where music, comedy, and drama take center stage. Attend symphonic performances, comedy plays, and live music events that reflect the region's diverse cultural environment.

3. Stroud Subscription Rooms

Embrace a range of artistic styles at Stroud Subscription Rooms, a facility that offers a platform for live music, comedy, drama, and more. Experience the intimacy of smaller events and interact with the local arts community.

4. Cotswold Playhouse, Stroud

Journey to Cotswold Playhouse in Stroud, a theater that celebrates local talent and originality. Witness a mix of theatrical plays, from thought-provoking tragedies to light hearted comedies, in an intimate environment that improves the theatrical experience.

5. Sudeley Castle Outdoor Performances

Experience the wonder of live performances against the setting of old Sudeley Castle. Attend outdoor concerts, theatrical shows, and cultural events that merge the grandeur of the castle's grounds with the appeal of artistic expression.

6. Festivals and Cultural Events

Throughout the year, the Cotswolds offers a number of festivals and cultural events that highlight the performing arts. From music festivals to literary meetings, immerse yourself in the region's culture tapestry and interact with kindred lovers.

7. Music and Folk Clubs

Explore local music and folk groups that offer an insight into the region's musical practices. Join jam sessions, folk nights, and live music events to uncover the heartfelt sounds that reverberate inside the Cotswolds.

8. Practical Suggestions

Event Listings and Tickets: Stay updated about future performances by checking event listings on official websites or local publications. Purchase tickets in advance to protect your position at shows.

Venue Accessibility: Check the accessibility of performing arts venues and inquire about seating choices for those with special needs. Many sites offer accommodations to guarantee a comfortable experience for all participants.

Dining & Refreshments: Many performing arts venues feature on-site dining options or are located near nearby restaurants. Consider eating a meal or refreshments before or after a concert.

Local Culture and customs: Engage with local culture and customs by seeing performances that exhibit folk music, dances, and artistic expressions unique to the Cotswolds.

Where Art Comes Alive

Cotswolds Performing Arts Venues are more than locations for entertainment; they're platforms for storytelling, for musical journeys, and for the wonder of live shows. As you take your seat and the lights dim, you'll become a part of a shared experience, where the creative energy of the Cotswolds intertwines with the skills of performers. The performing arts venues allow you to cheer, to interact, and to take the melodies and emotions of each performance with you as you explore the Cotswolds.

3.4.3 Local Artisan Shops and Studios

Welcome to the Cotswolds, a location where the spirit of craftsmanship and artistic brilliance survives in the hands of local craftspeople. Amidst the charming villages and breathtaking surroundings, you'll uncover a treasure trove of artisan stores and workshops that offer a look into the Cotswolds' creative heart. As you enter into these havens of workmanship, you'll be immersed in a world of handmade treasures, meticulous designs, and the stories that breathe life into each item. Join us on an immersive excursion through Cotswolds Local Artisan Shops and Studios, where each design, brushstroke, and craftwork shows the region's enthusiasm for creativity and expertise.

1. Cotswold Pottery

Explore the art of pottery at Cotswold Pottery, where skilled potters mould clay into functional and artistic items. Witness the pottery-making process, from wheel throwing to glazing, and uncover unique works that represent the spirit of the Cotswolds.

2. Crafty Camping

Journey to Crafty Camping, a unique glamping facility that delivers more than just accommodation. Visit the on-site woodcraft workshop, where you may learn woodworking skills, build your own items, and interact with the natural beauty of the surroundings.

3. Cotswold Candle Company

Engage your senses at the Cotswold Candle Company, where hand-poured candles and handmade aromas lure you into a world of sensory enjoyment. Discover scents that evoke the beauty and experiences of the Cotswolds.

4. Cotswold Perfumery

Cotswold Perfumery is a perfumery where experienced perfumers create smells that capture the character of the location. Take a guided tour of the perfume-making process and even create your own signature smell.

5. Workshops and Classes for Artists

Many local craftspeople provide seminars and classes where you can learn about their crafts firsthand. Immerse yourself in creativity, from painting to jewelry making, and take home a bit of the artistic energy of the Cotswolds.

6. Woolen Weavers of the Cotswolds

Visit Cotswold Woolen Weavers, a historic mill that produces traditional woven fabrics, to immerse yourself in the world of textiles. Explore the weaving process, see beautiful designs, and shop for fabrics that highlight the textile history of the Cotswolds.

7. Tours of Galleries and Shops

Take gallery and store excursions that will present you to a wide range of local artists. These excursions, which range from glassblowers to woodworkers, provide insight into the craftsmanship that goes into each item.

8. Customized Souvenirs

Consider purchasing personalized mementos that reflect your experience when visiting local artist shops and studios. Custom-made crafts and artwork are treasured keepsakes from your trip.

9. Practical Suggestions

Studio visits: Plan your visits to artisan studios by checking their hours of operation and availability. Appointments may be required for guided tours or workshops at some studios.

Supporting Local Artisans: When you buy from a local artisan, you are directly supporting their trade as well as the creative community in the Cotswolds. Consider purchasing one-of-a-kind presents that capture the spirit of the location.

Engage with craftsmen by asking questions about their craft, inspiration, and processes. Many craftspeople are ready to share their expertise and enthusiasm with travelers.

Local Ingredients and Materials: Some artisans produce their crafts using materials obtained locally. Take note of the materials used in each piece and admire the link to the landscapes of the region.

Handmade Treasures

Local Artisan Shops & Studios in the Cotswolds are more than just places to shop; they're portals to creation, the artistry of human hands, and the stories that reinforce the region's cultural fabric. As you visit these artisans' havens, you'll become a part of a legacy that values history, creativity, and the magic of creation. The artisan stores and studios invite you to discover, interact with, and take home not only a created treasure, but a bit of the Cotswolds' character.

Outdoor Recreation

Welcome to the Cotswolds, where the great outdoors becomes your playground for adventure and discovery. This chapter will introduce you to a world of wonderful outdoor activities that will help you to connect with the region's natural beauty in new and exciting ways. The Cotswolds provide a variety of outdoor sports that suit every level of adventurer, from hiking along gorgeous routes to cycling experiences, from taking to the water in kayaks to soaring over the landscapes in hot air balloons. Join us as we explore the Cotswolds' outdoor activities, where each walk, paddle, and ascent provides an unforgettable experience that immerses you in nature's grandeur and the thrill of the great outdoors.

4.1 Trails for Hiking and Walking

4.1.1 National Trail of the Cotswolds

The Cotswold Way National Trail is a path that runs through the heart of the Cotswolds, providing a voyage of exploration, introspection, and connection with nature's splendor. As you begin this classic hiking trail, you'll pass through scenery that captures the soul of the region: rolling hills, charming villages, historic landmarks, and panoramic panoramas. This comprehensive experience transports you through time, revealing the layers of history, culture, and natural beauty that have created the Cotswolds into the delightful destination that it is today. Join us on an in-depth tour of the Cotswold Way National Trail, where each step becomes a journey into the essence of the Cotswolds and the stories embedded in its landscapes.

1. Chipping Campden is where it all starts.

The Cotswold Way adventure begins in the beautiful market town of Chipping Campden. As you begin the walk, you will be greeted with the classic Cotswold stone architecture and the promise of the experiences that await you.

2. Gentle Hills and Adorable Villages

The Cotswold Way takes you through a variety of settings, from gentle rolling hills to peaceful valleys. Along the way, you'll pass through towns that appear to be stuck in time, with thatched houses, inviting pubs, and the warm embrace of Cotswold hospitality.

3. Panorama Views from the Broadway Tower

Panorama views open before you as you climb Broadway Tower, a famous landmark. Enjoy stunning vistas of the Cotswold Hills, complete with patchwork farms and lovely towns straight out of a storybook.

4. Long Knap Belas Knap

Belas Knap, an ancient burial mound that predates the pyramids, transports you back in time. Discover this Neolithic site, where the whispers of the past become felt beneath your feet, and travel through time.

5. Sudeley Castle and Gardens are located in Sudeley, England.

Sudeley Castle's ancient splendor is situated within lovely grounds. Immerse yourself in royal stories, discover regal apartments, and walk through vibrant gardens reflecting centuries of cultivation.

6. Country Park Crickley Hill

Crickley Hill Country Park is a haven for nature's beauties. Explore forests, winding paths, and vantage spots with panoramic views of the surrounding landscape.

7. The Rococo Garden at Painswick

Visit Painswick Rococo Garden, a hidden gem displaying 18th-century garden design. Wander through colorful landscapes, discover elaborate follies, and immerse yourself in an artistic and calm environment.

8. Bath is where it all comes together.

The Cotswold Way concludes in Bath, a UNESCO World Heritage site famous for its Roman baths and Georgian buildings. Your journey comes to a conclusion amid the echoes of history and the vibrant pulse of city life.

9. Practical Suggestions

Research the trail's parts, distances, and elevations to personalize your trek to your preferences and fitness level. Plan ahead of time for lodging and food, especially during high seasons.

Wear comfortable, durable hiking footwear and dress in layers to deal with changeable conditions. Bring waterproof clothing, a hat, and sunscreen.

Navigation and Maps: Bring accurate trail maps, navigation software, or a hardcopy guidebook to keep you on track. The path is marked with signposts and signs, but being prepared is essential.

Lodgings and restock Points: Because lodgings vary along the trail, plan your overnight stays and restock points carefully. To completely immerse yourself in the Cotswold experience, consider staying at wonderful bed and breakfasts or inns.

Leave No Trace: Hike responsibly by following the Leave No Trace principles. Stay on authorized trails, properly dispose of rubbish, and respect the environment and local communities.

A Discovery Journey

The Cotswold Way National Trail is more than just a hike; it is a journey through time, environment, and the heart of the Cotswolds. Walking in the footsteps of ages past immerses you in a story that develops with each step—a story of beauty, tradition, and the human connection to the earth. The Cotswold Way encourages you to go on a journey of self-discovery, admiration for the landscape around you, and memories that will be inscribed in the fabric of your soul for the rest of your life.

Circular Walks in Several Villages

Welcome to the Cotswolds, an area of limitless beauty and calm that urges you to explore its hidden nooks via a series of enthralling circular walks. In this section, we'll walk you through a series of village-based treks that capture the essence of the Cotswolds on a small scale. Each circular trail takes you through attractive villages, scenic farmland, and local landmarks, providing a taste of the Cotswolds in manageable and picturesque doses. Join us on a journey of discovery, following in the footsteps of individuals who live in these communities and immersing ourselves in landscapes that have inspired generations.

1. Circular Walk in Bibury

Begin your journey at Bibury, a postcard-perfect village known for its honey-colored stone homes and idyllic environment. This round stroll follows the River Coln, past the well-known Arlington Row. Wander through flowery fields, cross historic stone bridges, and soak in the tranquil beauty that has enchanted artists and visitors alike.

2. Loops of Lower and Upper Slaughter

The Lower Slaughter and Upper Slaughter loops transport you to a storybook scene. Explore Lower Slaughter's lovely streets, which are decorated with quaint homes and a gently flowing river. Continue to Upper Slaughter, where the picturesque grounds and old church create a timeless atmosphere.

3. Circular Walk in Naunton

Discover the rustic charm of Naunton, a settlement in the Windrush Valley. This round trek takes you through a jumble of farmland, woods, and meadows. Follow the gentle contours of the terrain and soak up the tranquility that pervades this timeless Cotswold gem.

4. Ramble via Blockley and Moreton-in-Marsh

Begin your tour at Blockley, a community with a vibrant arts scene and a rich history. Travel through lush surroundings on your route to Moreton-in-Marsh, where you'll find a vibrant market area and old architecture. This ramble combines rural life with natural beauty.

5. The Discovery Walk in Chipping Campden

Explore Chipping Campden, a town where history and craftsmanship meet. Stroll around the town's historic High Street, admire its gorgeous architecture, and pay a visit to the magnificent St. James' Church. The adjacent countryside lends a scenic element to your exploration.

6. Route to Winchcombe and Sudeley Castle

Begin your journey at Winchcombe, a historic town that entices with its architecture and welcoming environment. This circular journey leads to Sudeley Castle's splendor, where gardens, history, and enthralling stories await. Make a day of it by exploring the town and the castle.

7. Practical Suggestions

Maps and Directions: Before embarking on each round trek, obtain complete maps and route explanations. Local visitor centers and guidebooks might provide useful information to help you navigate the roads effectively.

Footwear and attire: Wear comfortable walking shoes that are appropriate for the terrain. Dress in layers to accommodate changeable weather conditions, and carry sunscreen and a reusable water bottle.

Local Amenities: While traveling, look for local amenities such as restrooms, cafes, and shops. Prepare snacks and supplies ahead of time, especially in regions with restricted amenities.

Stay on established pathways, respect private property, and follow any signage or guidelines provided by the town or trail operators. Leave no evidence of your presence.

Engage with residents respectfully and inquire about the village's history, landmarks, and cultural activities. Support local businesses and craftspeople, and leave a positive impression on the towns you visit.

Circular walks in Cotswold villages provide more than just a stroll; they weave a tapestry of experiences from history, nature, and the warmth of local communities. Each village has its own narrative, its own distinct personality, and its own invitation to immerse yourself in the heart of the Cotswolds. As you meander through towns, cross bridges, and take in panoramic views, you'll realize that these circular walks are paths not merely through landscapes, but also through the core of what makes the Cotswolds so appealing.

4.2 Cycling Routes

Family-Friendly Cycling Routes

Welcome to the Cotswolds' world of riding, where breathtaking scenery, attractive towns, and family-friendly trails combine to offer an unforgettable bicycling experience. In this section, we'll walk you through a variety of family-friendly cycling routes, providing a relaxing and pleasurable ride for all ages. These trails promise the right blend of nature, culture, and family fun, whether you're going on a two-wheeled adventure with children or looking for a relaxed exploration of the countryside. Join us as we bike through the beauty of the Cotswolds and explore the joys of family-friendly cycling in this magnificent setting.

1. Cycle Route on the Cotswold Line

Take a bicycle tour along the Cotswold Line Cycle Route, which follows the route of the renowned Oxford-Worcester railway. This family-friendly route features low hills and a variety of landscapes, including meadows and woodlands. Stop at stops along the journey to learn about the history of the railway.

2. Honeybourne Line Cycling Path

Explore the Honeybourne route Cycle trail, a disused railway route that has been converted into a pleasant riding trail. With a smooth surface that winds through gorgeous scenery and charming villages, this trail is great for families. Take in the scenery and look for wildlife along the way.

3. Strawberry Line Cycling Route

Ride your bike along the Strawberry Line Cycle Route, which runs through the heart of the Cotswolds and provides stunning vistas of the Mendip Hills. With traffic-free sections and opportunities to explore attractive towns along the way, this route is ideal for families.

4. Windrush Valley Cycling Route

Discover the splendor of the Windrush Valley Cycle Route, a family-friendly path that takes you through the iconic landscapes of the Cotswolds. Pass through picturesque villages, meadows, and peaceful waterscapes on a leisurely ride suitable for all ages.

5. Practical Suggestions

Bike Rentals and Equipment: If you don't own a bike, try hiring one from a local bike shop or cycle hire company. Ensure that the bikes are correctly fitted and that there are enough for family members of different sizes.

Prioritize safety by wearing helmets, following traffic laws, and teaching youngsters basic riding etiquette. Wear bright clothing and use lights if cycling during low-light hours to stay visible.

Carry necessities like water, snacks, modest tools, and a first aid kit. Make sure everyone has enough sun protection, such as hats, sunglasses, and sunscreen.

Plan for many breaks along the journey to allow youngsters to rest, explore, and take in their surroundings. Many bike paths include designated rest stops and picnic places.

Before you head out, familiarize yourself with the route's distance, geography, and potential highlights. To keep on track and prevent getting lost, use maps or navigation apps.

Participate in local communities and observe any rules for riding through cities and villages. Respect private property and be considerate of pedestrians and other bicycles.

Wonder Wheeling

Cycling in the Cotswolds with your family is a journey of discovery, shared experiences, and the pure delight of biking through landscapes straight out of a storybook. You'll create memories that weave together the beauty of nature and the warmth of family togetherness as you cycle through traffic-free pathways, through quaint villages, and past landscapes that spread like paintings. The family-friendly cycling routes invite you to explore, bond, and weave a tapestry of memories that will be woven into the fabric of your Cotswold experience.

4.2.2 Difficult Cycling Routes for Enthusiasts

Welcome to the thrilling world of tough cycling routes in the Cotswolds, where adventurers and enthusiasts may test their boundaries and enjoy the thrill of the ride. In this section, we'll look at a variety of routes that will put your stamina, ability, and the simple thrill of overcoming difficult terrain to the test. These routes cater to experienced riders wanting an adrenaline rush amidst the region's magnificent surroundings, with steep climbs and difficult descents. Join us as we gear up, cycle hard, and enjoy the heart-pounding pleasure of difficult cycling in the Cotswolds.

1. Loop Cotswold Edge

Set out on the Cotswold Edge Loop, a challenging course that takes you over undulating terrain, high climbs, and spectacular descents. The circle provides panoramic views of the Cotswold Hills, rewarding your efforts with breath-taking scenery.

2. Broadway Tower Climb

Take on the Broadway Tower Challenge, a course that puts your strength to the test with a climb to the famed Broadway Tower. The ascent rewards you with panoramic views of the countryside, while the rapid fall adds a thrilling element to your adventure.

3. Coopers Hill and Birdlip Ride

Prepare for the Birdlip and Coopers Hill Ride, a difficult circuit with hills, steep descents, and meandering paths. The route shows the different terrain of the Cotswolds, from woodlands to open fields, and provides a wonderful riding experience.

4. Circular Road from Winchcombe to Stanway

Set off on the Winchcombe to Stanway Circular, a route that has both hard hills and spectacular descent sections. You'll see ancient buildings, lovely cities, and the joy of overcoming difficult terrain as you ride through picturesque landscapes.

5. Practical Suggestions

Physical Preparation: Before embarking on difficult cycling routes, make sure you're physically prepared for the demands of steep ascents, technical descents, and varied terrain. Cycling ability can be improved by regular training and conditioning.

Bike Maintenance: Inspect your bike's condition, including the brakes, gears, and tires, to ensure it is in good operating order. To ensure safety and efficiency, technical routes necessitate well-maintained equipment.

Wear appropriate safety equipment, such as helmets, gloves, and protective clothes. Familiarize yourself with the route's challenges, potential hazards, and high-risk places.

Before you leave, familiarize yourself with the route map, elevation profiles, and essential locations. To keep on track, carry a GPS device or a navigation app, and consider sharing your itinerary with a friend or family member.

Hydration and nutrition: Keep hydrated by carrying enough water, especially on physically taxing journeys. Pack energy-dense snacks to keep your body fueled and your energy levels up.

Respect for Nature: Ride your bike safely, staying on marked pathways and avoiding fragile ecosystems and protected areas. Respect the environment and the local people by leaving no evidence of your presence.

The Cotswold Trails

Cycling routes in the Cotswolds are more than just a physical challenge; they are a voyage of triumph, self-discovery, and the pure delight of tackling difficult terrain. As you tackle hills, handle technical sections, and descend with exhilaration, you'll be immersed in a world that combines adrenaline with natural beauty. The demanding cycling routes urge you to test your boundaries, relish every hard-earned victory, and leave a path of memories that represent your tenacious spirit of adventure.

4.3 Equestrian and Horse Riding Experiences

Welcome to the world of horseback riding and equestrian activities in the Cotswolds, where the cadence of hoofbeats echoes the natural beauty and historic charm of the region. In this section, we'll walk you through a variety of horseback riding opportunities that will allow you to explore the landscapes of the Cotswolds on the back of a gorgeous horse. These experiences, which range from leisurely hacks around lovely villages to immersive equestrian instruction, provide a unique viewpoint and a profound connection with the area. Join us as we mount our horses and embark on a journey that combines tradition, nature, and the excitement of equestrian adventure.

1. Horseback Riding Tours with a Guide

Guided riding tours offered by local stables and equestrian schools allow you to explore the Cotswolds on horseback. Experienced guides walk you along gorgeous paths, providing history, natural landmarks, and hidden gems. Select from a variety of tours ranging from short rides to full-day experiences.

2. Equestrian Centre of Bourton Vale

The Bourton Vale Equestrian Centre is located in the heart of the Cotswolds. This recognized facility provides horseback riding lessons and hacking adventures for riders of all abilities. From novice to advanced riders, you'll have the opportunity to explore the breathtaking scenery while honing your riding skills.

3. Cotswold Hills Horseback Riding

Set out on a horseback ride in the Cotswold Hills, where wide landscapes and bridle lanes beckon. Hike through undulating meadows, forests, and historic towns on routes that loop through rolling meadows, forests, and historic towns. As you connect with nature, enjoy the flow of your horse's movement.

4. Riding Lessons on Your Own

Individual riding sessions taught by skilled teachers can help you improve your equestrian skills. Whether you're a beginner or looking to improve your technique, individualized courses offer one-on-one guidance and a tailored learning experience.

5. Equestrian Vacations

Take an equestrian holiday that combines riding and relaxing. Select from a variety of packages that include lodging, guided rides, and equestrian activities. Every day, take in the beauty of the Cotswolds from a different angle.

6. Horse Riding Etiquette and Safety

Appropriate Attire: Dress comfortably for horseback riding, such as long pants, closed-toe shoes, and a riding helmet. Hats are frequently provided by stables, although you are welcome to bring your own if you prefer.

Rider Experience Level: When booking horseback riding activities, be honest about your riding experience. This ensures that you are paired with the appropriate horse and trail for your ability level.

Horses should be treated with kindness and care. To protect the safety and well-being of both riders and horses, follow the instructions of guides and instructors.

Advance Reservations: Plan ahead of time for horseback riding trips, especially during busy seasons. Confirm the experience's specifics, such as length, group size, and any special requirements.

Trotting Through Tradition

Horseback riding and equestrian adventures in the Cotswolds are more than just a ride; they are a voyage of connection, a mix of history, and a tapestry of nature's beauty. You'll see the Cotswolds from a different perspective as you ride past quaint villages, along bridle roads, and through landscapes that have withstood the test of time. The horse riding experiences invite you to interact, learn, and create memories that mix the majesty of horses with the appeal of the breathtaking surroundings of the Cotswolds.

4.4 Hot Air Balloon Rides

Welcome to the thrilling world of Cotswolds hot air balloon rides, where the sky becomes your canvas and the landscapes below unfurl in magnificent grandeur. In this part, we'll walk you through the thrilling experience of flying through the skies in a hot air balloon, providing a new perspective on the beauty and charm of the Cotswolds. Hot air balloon tours promise a once-in-a-lifetime journey that elevates your relationship with the region's surroundings, from the peaceful excitement of the climb to the awe-inspiring panoramas that stretch beneath you. Join us as we climb, float, and marvel at the Cotswolds' infinite magnificence from above.

1. Companies that operate hot air balloons

Choose from a number of reliable hot air balloon businesses in the Cotswolds. Investigate their offers, safety records, and customer feedback to find a firm that gives a safe and pleasant experience.

2. Getting Ready for the Flight

Arrive at the designated meeting spot at the scheduled hour on the day of your hot air balloon flight. The ballooning crew will give you safety instructions, a brief summary of the flight experience, and will answer any questions you may have.

3. Ascending to the Heavens

Feel the serene sensation of rising above the ground as you climb in the hot air balloon. Feel the calm breeze as you leave the Earth behind and go on a voyage that will provide you with a new perspective of the landscapes of the Cotswolds.

4. Awe-Inspiring Sceneries

Admire the spectacular views that unfold beneath you from your vantage point high above. The Cotswold Hills, charming towns, and winding rivers form a breathtaking panorama that embodies the soul of the region.

5. Serenity Floating

Feel the peace of flying across the skies as the hot air balloon follows the wind currents. The weightlessness and tranquility of the flight produce an extraordinary sensation that connects you to the beauty of the Cotswolds in a fresh and profound way.

6. Celebration and Landing

The hot air balloon will descend to a suitable landing site after an enjoyable flight. The experienced flight crew will direct the landing, assuring your safety and comfort. After landing, salute your voyage with a classic Champagne toast, a time-honored ballooning tradition.

7. Practical Suggestions

Considerations for the Weather: Hot air balloon trips are weather-dependent, with wind speed, direction, and visibility all having a part in flight operations. Prepare for the possibility of postponing due to inclement weather.

Wear comfortable attire appropriate for the weather circumstances, as temperatures above may differ from those on the ground. Wearing loose scarves or accessories that could become entangled during the trip is not recommended.

Camera & Memories: Bring your camera or smartphone to capture the breathtaking views and moments of your hot air balloon flight. Be wary of fastening your camera, as windy conditions in the air might make gadget handling problematic.

Safety first: Always follow the ballooning team's instructions, especially during takeoff and landing. Pay close attention to safety briefings and follow any safety instructions that are stated.

Hot air balloon rides are popular and may necessitate ahead planning. Plan your ride in advance to ensure a spot on a specific date and time.

The Sky's Adoration

Hot air balloon rides are more than just a trip; they are an embrace of the sky, a dance with the wind, and a voyage that elevates your relationship with the stunning beauty of the Cotswolds. You'll feel the region's attraction in a way that surpasses the ordinary as you soar above the sights that have captured hearts for millennia. The hot air balloon journey invites you to let go, climb, and create memories that capture the freedom of flight and the timeless magnificence of the Cotswolds.

Excellent firms to pick from

In the Cotswolds, there are a few reliable hot air balloon businesses that provide flights. Please keep in mind that availability and offerings are subject to change, so it's best to check their websites or contact them directly for the most up-to-date information and to book your reservation:

Cotswold Balloon Safaris: Website: cotswoldballoonsafaris.co.uk Known for: Exclusive hot air balloon adventures with customized care, with a focus on small groups for a more intimate experience.

Cotswold Ballooning: Website: cotswold-flying.co.uk Known for: Offering flights over the gorgeous Cotswold environment, offering the opportunity to observe historic buildings and lovely towns from above.

Cotswold Hot Air Balloon Rides: Website: cotswoldhotairballoonrides.com Known for: Offering hot air balloon rides that capture the spirit of the beauty and charm of the Cotswolds.

Ballooning Network: Website: ballooningnetwork.com Known for: Providing a network of balloon ride providers, allowing you to choose from many Cotswolds launch points.

Balloons over the Cotswolds: Website: balloonsoverthecotswolds.co.uk Known for: Offering balloon flights over the rolling hills and charming towns of the Cotswolds, accompanied by expert pilots.

BlueSky Balloons: Website: blueskyballoons.co.uk Known for: Providing hot air balloon rides with stunning views of the Cotswold countryside, led by professional pilots.

Please keep in mind to check the websites of the providers for information on flight availability, pricing, duration, and any special offers. It's also a good idea to check customer reviews and comments to get a sense of their experiences. Whether you're searching for a romantic getaway, a family adventure, or a solo flight, these companies have a variety of options to help you make the most of your Cotswolds hot air balloon experience.

4.5 Golf Courses in Beautiful Locations

Welcome to the world of golf in the Cotswolds, where lush fairways, picturesque scenery, and peaceful settings provide the ideal setting for a day on the green. In this section, we'll walk you through a selection of golf courses located inside stunning settings, allowing you to enjoy the sport while taking in the region's natural beauty. These golfing destinations offer an exquisite retreat for golfers of all levels, from demanding courses to relaxed rounds. Join us as we tour the greens, make tee dates, and enjoy the peace and quiet of Cotswolds golf.

1. The Golf Club at Manor House

This course, located inside the opulent surroundings of The Manor House Hotel and Golf Club, provides a superb golfing experience. Tee off against the gorgeous backdrop of the Wiltshire countryside, with challenging holes that will put your talents to the test while immersing you in tranquility.

2. Golf Club Minchinhampton

Discover the beauty of Minchinhampton Golf Club, which features three courses. The Old Course, The Avening Course, and The Cherington Course all provide varying degrees of difficulty and are situated against the gorgeous Cotswold environment.

3. Naunton Downs Golf Course

Play a round of golf at Naunton Downs Golf Club, which is located in the heart of the Cotswolds. The course is well-known for its scenic vistas of the surrounding countryside, making it a tranquil location for golfers seeking both challenge and leisure.

4. Cotswold Hills Golf Club is a golf club in the Cotswolds.

Tee off at Cotswold Hills Golf Club, where undulating fairways and well-kept greens provide a traditional golfing experience. The elevation location of the course provides panoramic vistas of the Cotswold Hills, offering a stunning backdrop for your game.

5. Reservations for Tee Times

Online Reservations: The majority of golf courses have online booking systems that allow you to select your chosen tee times and courses. To access the various golf club booking services, go to their respective websites.

Phone Reservations: For a more personalized experience, call the golf club's booking line to inquire about tee times, course conditions, and any special deals.

Advance Booking: To assure availability and secure your preferred tee times, consider booking in advance, especially during high golfing seasons.

6. Getting Ready for Your Round

Golf gear should include collared shirts, appropriate slacks or shorts, and golf shoes with soft spikes. Check with the golf course to see if there are any unique dress code restrictions.

Equipment Rentals: If you are traveling without your golf clubs, most golf courses provide club, golf cart, and pull cart rentals.

Course Information: Learn the layout of the course, including the yardage of each hole and any potential hazards. Course manuals and scorecards are frequently available at the clubhouse of a golf course.

7. Best Golfing Techniques

tempo of Play: To provide a great experience for all participants, respect the tempo of play. Maintain a steady pace and stay up with the group ahead of you throughout the round.

Golf Course Etiquette: Follow golf course etiquette by repairing divots, raking bunkers, and replacing ball marks on the green. Keep noise levels to a minimum to respect other players' concentration.

Environmental Stewardship: Protect the course's natural beauty by minimizing unnecessary damage to plants and wildlife. Respect any environmental standards and stay on approved walkways.

The Swinging Art

Golf courses in magnificent Cotswold surroundings offer more than just a game; they offer an artistic fusion of sport, tranquillity, and relationship with the environment. You'll see the Cotswolds from a different perspective as you line up your photo, feel the breeze on your face, and take in the beauty that surrounds you. The golf courses invite you to test yourself, establish your rhythm, and create memories that represent the sport's beauty and the timeless allure of the Cotswolds.

Local Dining and Cuisine

5.1 Cotswold Cuisine Overview

Welcome to the Cotswolds' gourmet journey, where flavors steeped in tradition and local ingredients weave a tapestry of culinary enjoyment. In this section, we'll walk you through the core of Cotswold cuisine, from substantial dishes to treats that highlight the region's wealth. Every meal tells a tale as you explore the local dining scene—a story of legacy, craftsmanship, and a profound connection to the land. Join us on a culinary expedition as we immerse ourselves in the flavors, textures, and stories that define Cotswold food.

1. The Heartbeat of Local Ingredients

Cotswold gastronomy highlights the region's farms, meadows, and orchards. Ingredients acquired locally take center stage, reflecting the rhythm of the seasons and the harmony between people and environment. Each dish is a monument to the land's generosity, from fresh vegetables and artisanal cheeses to grass-fed meats and hand-picked herbs.

2. Tradition's Flavours

Cotswold cuisine pays attention to tradition by using recipes passed down through generations. You'll come across delicacies that have been painstakingly maintained and adored over time. Enjoy pies laden with exquisite meats, puddings that warm the heart, and stews that provide warmth on a cold day.

3. A Taste of History

Every dish in Cotswold cuisine is infused with a bit of the region's history. The food conveys the story of old trade routes, medieval markets, and the resourcefulness of farmers and cooks who adapted to their environment. Enjoy delicacies that have adorned tables for centuries while learning about the history of Cotswold cuisine.

4. Savoring Cotswold Delicacies

Start your day with a traditional Cotswold farmhouse breakfast, replete with locally sourced bacon, sausages, eggs, mushrooms, tomatoes, and black pudding. It's a filling and delightful way to fuel your journey.

Cotswold Lamb: Savor luscious Cotswold lamb raised on local farms. From roast lamb dinners to slow-cooked stews, the soft meat is frequently included in dishes that highlight its inherent flavor.

Double Gloucester Cheese: Savour the creamy goodness of Double Gloucester cheese, a local delicacy with a long history. This cheese adds a distinct Cotswold flavor to dishes, whether eaten alone or in combination.

Fruit-Forward Desserts: Indulge in desserts that highlight the region's farms. Cotswold desserts, from apple pies to berry crumbles, celebrate the sweetness of nature's bounty.

5. Visiting Local Restaurants

Dine in historic pubs that have been welcoming tourists and locals for generations. These establishments have a cozy atmosphere and menus that feature traditional Cotswold dishes.

Farm-to-Table Restaurants: Learn about farm-to-table restaurants that emphasize fresh, local ingredients in their dishes. Enjoy meals that highlight the flavors of the season as well as the skill of local chefs.

Tea Rooms and Bakeries: Indulge in afternoon tea or visit local bakeries to sample Cotswold-inspired pastries, cakes, and treats. For a traditional experience, pair your tea with freshly baked scones and clotted cream.

6. Participate in Food Festivals

Participate in local food festivals celebrating Cotswold cuisine. These events highlight the region's best foods, culinary traditions, and the camaraderie of communities coming together to share a passion for good food.

7. Dining that is environmentally friendly

Cotswold cuisine is compatible with environmentally friendly practices that respect the land and its resources. Many local restaurants emphasize locally sourced, seasonal ingredients, lowering carbon footprints and supporting local producers.

A Traditional Feast

Cotswold cuisine is a feast of tradition, a celebration of heritage, and a communion with the land. As you savor each bite, you'll notice that the flavors evoke memories of the past, artisans' skill, and the joy of sharing food with loved ones. Cotswold cuisine invites you to taste, reminisce, and create memories that combine the culinary arts with the area's timeless allure.

5.2 Traditional Public Houses and Gastropubs

Welcome to the heart of Cotswold dining, where centuries-old pubs and gastropubs blend historic charm with modern culinary excellence. In this section, we'll take you on a tour of the vibrant world of Cotswold pubs, where hearty meals, local brews, and conviviality mingle in a warm and welcoming environment. These pubs offer a taste of history and a glimpse into the soul of the region, from the crackling fireplace to the hearty fare. Join us as we enter cozy pubs, raise a glass, and sample the flavors that define Cotswold pub culture.

1. The Heart of Cotswold Pubs

Cotswold pubs are more than just places to eat and drink; they are cultural landmarks that encapsulate the region's spirit. These pubs offer a glimpse into the past while accepting the present with their rustic interiors, wooden beams, and welcoming ambiance.

2. Traditional Pub Food

Indulge in traditional Cotswold pub fare that both warms the soul and satisfies the palate. The menus are a celebration of comfort food at its best, with everything from hearty pies and fish and chips to steak and ale stew.

3. Local Ales and Drinks

Raise a glass of Cotswold ale, cider, or gin to the rich tapestry of Cotswold beverages. Many pubs feature a variety of regional beers that complement the flavors of the food.

4. The Modern Take on Gastropubs

Gastropubs modernize traditional pub dining by providing refined culinary experiences in a pub setting. Expect unique dishes, locally sourced ingredients, and inventive combinations that pay homage to Cotswold flavors.

5. Visiting Cotswold Pubs

Discover The Feathered Nest Country Inn, a gastropub known for its fine food and picturesque setting. This restaurant in Nether Westcote offers seasonal menus, fine wines, and panoramic views.

The Swan Inn: Visit The Swan Inn, a charming pub in the heart of Bibury. Its thatched roof and riverside location make it ideal for enjoying traditional dishes and relaxing by the water.

The Wild Rabbit: The Wild Rabbit is a gastropub in Kingham that focuses on sustainable and locally sourced foods. This Michelin-starred restaurant combines elegance and Cotswold charm.

6. Pub Manners

Table Service: Table service is available in some Cotswold pubs, where staff will take your order at your table. Others may require you to place your order at the bar.

Tipping is customary in Cotswold pubs. While gratuities are not required, they are appreciated for excellent service.

Menus are typically displayed on chalkboards or given on paper when ordering food. Depending on the pub's style, order your food and drinks at the bar or wait for table service.

7. Local Happenings and Live Music

Local events, quiz nights, and live music are frequently held in Cotswold bars. Look for special evenings that allow you to mingle with locals and experience the lively pub scene.

Traditional pubs and gastropubs in the Cotswolds provide more than just a meal; they offer a taste of Cotswold kindness, a mingling of flavors, and an immersion in local culture. As you enter these historic establishments, you'll notice that the warmth of the fire, the clink of glasses, and hearty laughter echo the timeless allure of pub life. Cotswold pubs invite you to dine, converse, and create memories that are intertwined with the area's history and conviviality.

5.3 Restaurants Serving Fine Dining

Welcome to Cotswolds fine dining, where artistry and gastronomy combine to create unforgettable culinary experiences. In this section, we'll take you on a tour of the finest restaurants in the Cotswolds, where creativity, innovation, and attention to detail transform meals into masterpieces. These restaurants offer a journey into the heart of Cotswold flavors elevated to the level of art, with exquisite tasting menus and impeccable service. Join us as we enter refined rooms, savor each course, and revel in the elegance that is synonymous with Cotswold fine dining.

1. The Flavor Symphony

Cotswold fine dining establishments are flavor symphonies, orchestrating ingredients into harmonious compositions that tantalize the senses. Each dish demonstrates the chef's mastery, demonstrating a fusion of tradition and innovation.

2. Ingredients from artisans

The Cotswolds' fine dining celebrates the region's artisanal ingredients, which are sourced from local farms, farmers, and markets. Each ingredient, from organic vegetables to sustainably caught seafood, is chosen with precision and care.

3. Menus de dégustation

Taste the artistry of tasting menus that take you on a culinary journey. These menus frequently include a number of small plates, allowing you to sample a wide range of flavors and textures in a single meal.

4. Cotswold Fine Dining Treasures

Discover Le Champignon Sauvage, a Michelin-starred restaurant in Cheltenham known for its inventive French-inspired cuisine. Chef David Everitt-Matthias creates tasting menus with seasonal ingredients.

Whatley Manor: Enjoy an upscale hotel and restaurant in Malmesbury at Whatley Manor. Whatley Manor's Dining Room provides a refined dining experience with a focus on locally sourced foods.

Lords of the Manor: Lords of the Manor is a one-of-a-kind hotel and restaurant in Upper Slaughter. The Michelin-starred restaurant serves modern British cuisine inspired by the bounty of the Cotswolds.

5. Reservation Protocol

Reservations are often required for fine dining restaurants, especially for tasting menus and special dining events. To ensure your preferred date and time, reserve your table well in advance.

Special Requests: Please notify the restaurant when making your reservation if you have any dietary restrictions or preferences. They will frequently adjust to your requirements to ensure a memorable dining experience.

6. The Dress Code

Many of the best restaurants in the Cotswolds have a smart casual or formal dress code. Check the restaurant's dress code to ensure you're appropriately attired for your dining experience.

7. Sommeliers and Wine Pairing

Wine pairings suggested by knowledgeable sommeliers will enhance your fine dining experience. The wine list is carefully curated to complement each dish, resulting in a harmonious blend of flavors.

Epicurean Canvas

Fine dining restaurants in the Cotswolds provide more than just a meal; they provide an epicurean canvas, a world where taste, presentation, and ambiance all come together to create an emotional feast. As you begin your culinary journey, you'll discover that the elegance of the surroundings, the artistry of the dishes, and the attentiveness of the service combine to create an experience that goes beyond mere dining. Cotswold fine dining invites you to savor, admire, and create memories that reflect the area's grace and sophistication.

5.4 Teahouses and Cafés

Welcome to the heartwarming world of Cotswold tea rooms and cafés, where quaint settings, delectable treats, and steaming cups of tea beckon you to unwind and savor life's simple pleasures. In this section, we'll take you on a tour of the charms of tea rooms and cafés, where moments of relaxation and connection are enhanced by the aroma of freshly brewed tea and the sweetness of pastries. From traditional cream teas to artisanal coffees, these establishments provide a cozy haven amidst the beauty of the Cotswolds. Join us as we enter inviting spaces, take a seat by the window, and enjoy the comforts of Cotswold culinary culture.

1. The Tea and Coffee Craft

Tea rooms and cafés in the Cotswolds are more than just places to get a drink; they are places where the art of tea and coffee is celebrated. Every cup is lovingly brewed, and every sip is a reminder to slow down and enjoy the moment.

2. Cream Tea from the Cotswolds

Indulge in the time-honored tradition of Cotswold cream tea, which includes freshly baked scones with whipped cream and jam. The combination of flavors—sweet, creamy, and fruity—is a classic Cotswold experience.

3. Coffees and Blends Made by Hand

Cafés in the Cotswolds serve artisanal coffee blends created by skilled baristas. Enjoy the complex aromas and flavors of single-origin coffees that have been expertly brewed to perfection.

4. Pastries, Cakes, and Sweets

Tea rooms and cafés in the Cotswolds serve a variety of pastries, cakes, and treats to go with your hot drink. From buttery croissants to decadent cakes, these treats pair perfectly with your beverage.

5. Tea Rooms and Cafés in the Cotswolds

Lavender Bakehouse: In Chalford, Lavender Bakehouse serves homemade cakes, pastries, and light meals. The bakery's charming garden setting contributes to the relaxed atmosphere.

Lucy's Tea Room: Visit Lucy's Tea Room in Stow-on-the-Wold for traditional cream teas and home-baked cakes. The vintage décor and welcoming atmosphere make it a tourist favorite.

Huffkins: Huffkins is a Cotswold institution with locations in various towns. Huffkins captures the essence of Cotswold charm with its traditional afternoon teas and exceptional baked goods.

6. Local Flavors and Ingredients

Many Cotswolds tea rooms and cafés emphasize locally sourced ingredients and flavors. Each bite carries a piece of the Cotswold scenery, from honey harvested in nearby apiaries to fruit preserves made with regional produce.

7. Ambience and Community

Tea rooms and cafés provide more than just refreshments; they are also relaxing and social places. The soft lighting, comfortable seating, and friendly staff create an atmosphere in which you can linger and unwind.

Culinary Pleasures

Tea rooms and cafés in the Cotswolds provide more than just a drink; they also provide culinary comforts, a relaxing haven, and a taste of home away from home. The clinking of teacups and the hum of conversation echo the timeless appeal of leisurely moments as you enter these charming establishments. Cotswold tea rooms and cafés invite you to sip, savor, and create memories that reflect the region's warmth and contentment.

5.5 Farmers' Markets and Local Produce

Welcome to the vibrant world of farmers' markets and local food in the Cotswolds, where the bounty of the land takes center stage. In this section, we'll explore the allure of farmers' markets, where stalls brimming with fresh ingredients, artisanal products, and handcrafted crafts weave a tapestry of flavors and traditions. These markets offer a direct link to the region's agricultural history, with everything from seasonal fruits and vegetables to artisan cheeses and homemade preserves. Join us as we stroll through bustling stalls, meet local producers, and immerse ourselves in the Cotswolds' rich harvest.

1. A View of Rural Life

Farmers' markets in the Cotswolds offer a glimpse into the heart of rural life, where the offerings of the stands are shaped by the rhythms of the land. These markets honor the region's agricultural history as well as the hard work of local farmers and artisans.

2. Seasonal Favorites

Visit farmers' markets to experience the joy of seasonal produce. Each season delivers a fresh assortment of flavors to taste and appreciate, from spring's brilliant greens to autumn's apples and pumpkins.

3. Offerings from Artists

Farmers' markets sell artisanal items ranging from handcrafted cheeses and cured meats to freshly baked bread and pastries. These offerings demonstrate the abilities and dedication of local producers.

4. Getting to Know Local Producers

Interact with local producers to meet the people behind the goods. Learn about their techniques, traditions, and the stories that inspire their work.

5. Farmers' Markets in the Cotswolds

Stroud Farmers' Market: One of the most well-known markets in the Cotswolds is Stroud Farmers' Market. This award-winning market offers a wide variety of vendors selling anything from organic veggies to handcrafted goods.

Cirencester Farmers' Market: Shop for fresh veggies, local meats, and handmade cheeses at the Cirencester Farmers' Market. The market's location in the historic market town adds to its allure.

Moreton-in-Marsh Farmers' Market: On the first Tuesday of each month, visit the Moreton-in-Marsh Farmers' Market. Discover a variety of local goods, such as baked goods, fresh flowers, and crafts.

6. Engaging with Sustainability

Farmers' markets in the Cotswolds generally stress sustainable techniques. Many of the items available are cultivated, bred, or crafted with an eye toward minimizing environmental impact.

7. Inspiration for Cooking

Farmers' markets not only provide the opportunity to purchase fresh ingredients, but they also inspire culinary inventiveness. Imagine the recipes you can make with the vivid selection of vegetables and products as you browse the stalls.

A Connection Feast

Farmers' markets and local food in the Cotswolds offer more than a shopping experience; they provide a feast of connection, a direct link between the land and the table. As you walk among the stalls, the scents of ripe fruits, the colors of seasonal veggies, and the friendliness of fellow customers reflect the eternal allure of community and sustenance. Farmers' markets in the Cotswolds enable you to discover, engage, and create memories that reflect the abundance and authenticity of the region.

The Cotswolds are a great place to go shopping.

6.1 Souvenirs and Local Crafts

Welcome to the magical world of Cotswold shopping, where hidden jewels and valued keepsakes await your discovery. In this region, we'll walk you through the domain of souvenirs and local crafts, where the skill of Cotswold artists is exhibited in every production. From handcrafted ceramics to complex textiles, these gems encapsulate the soul of the region's history and inventiveness. Join us as we find beautiful stores, meet skilled craftsmen, and immerse ourselves in the rich tapestry of Cotswold shopping.

1. Artistry in Every Detail

Souvenirs and local crafts in the Cotswolds are more than simple trinkets—they are reflections of the region's culture and past. Each piece showcases the talents, traditions, and craftsmanship of Cotswold craftspeople.

2. Handcrafted Ceramics

Discover the beauty of handcrafted ceramics that bear the imprint of Cotswold inventiveness. From delicate pottery to durable mugs, these items are inspired by the landscapes, vegetation, and fauna of the area.

3. Textiles & Fabrics

Experience the charm of textiles and materials that exhibit the Cotswolds' artistic character. Browse through exquisite tapestries, woven blankets, and embroidered linens that catch the spirit of the land.

4. Local Artisanal Goods

Cotswold shopping offers a wide assortment of artisanal goods, from hand-poured candles and scented soaps to expertly produced leather goods and unusual jewelry. These things make for thoughtful keepsakes that evoke the beauty of the location.

5. Exploring Cotswold Boutiques

Cotswold Trading: Visit Cotswold Trading, a store that curates an outstanding assortment of homeware, gifts, and accessories. Here, you'll find a choice of locally crafted and globally inspired gifts.

Daylesford Organic Farm Shop: Experience Daylesford Organic Farm Shop, a destination that offers organic produce, artisanal items, and home furnishings. Explore the shop's variety of finely crafted products that reflect the Cotswold lifestyle.

The Malthouse Collective: Discover The Malthouse Collective, a treasure trove of antiques, vintage discoveries, and artisanal goods. This unique group exhibits the work of local artists and craftspeople.

6. Supporting Local Artisans

When you buy souvenirs and crafts in the Cotswolds, you're not simply purchasing a memento—you're supporting the livelihoods of local artisans and adding to the sustainability of the region's creative community.

7. Preserving Heritage

Many local crafts and souvenirs pay homage to the Cotswolds' rich past. Whether inspired by historical architecture, local flora and fauna, or traditional techniques, these creations retain the region's legacy.

Artful Remembrances

Souvenirs and local crafts in the Cotswolds offer more than keepsakes; they provide creative remembrances, visual parts of the region's personality. As you browse the shelves, the textures of ceramics, the vibrancy of textiles, and the stories of workmanship echo the enduring fascination of creativity and authenticity. Cotswold shopping invites you to gaze, to purchase, and to make memories that mirror the richness and creativity of the area.

6.2 Antiques & Vintage Shops

Welcome to the world of Cotswolds antiques and vintage shops, where the echoes of history vibrate in every room. In this part, we'll walk you through the fascination of antiques and vintage shops, where hidden jewels, heirlooms, and curiosities await your discovery. From antique furniture that recalls tales of years gone by to vintage clothes that emanates timeless elegance, these boutiques provide a voyage into the past. Join us as we wander inside lovely emporiums, browse dusty shelves, and find the treasures that define Cotswolds rich heritage.

1. Echoes of the Past

Antiques and vintage shops in the Cotswolds are repository of stories, where artifacts from bygone times find new life and new admirers. Each piece carries the weight of history, a tribute to the lives and times that came before.

2. Antique Furniture

Discover the charm of antique furniture that fills the showrooms of Cotswold's businesses. From finely carved wooden pieces to timeless cushioned chairs, these furniture are reminiscent of a bygone elegance.

3. Vintage Clothing and Accessories

Experience the splendor of vintage garments and accessories that evoke the fashion of yesteryears. Browse through racks of clothing that catch the essence of different decades and bring a touch of nostalgia.

4. Collectibles and Curiosities

Antiques and vintage shops are treasure troves of rarities and curiosities that cater to varied preferences. From porcelain figures and vintage cameras to beautiful china sets, these objects offer individuality to any collection.

5. Exploring Cotswold's Antique & Vintage Shops

The Malthouse Collective: Visit The Malthouse Collective, a site that houses a varied assortment of antiques, vintage objects, and handcrafted products. Here, you'll find remarkable objects that narrate stories of the past.

Stow Antiques: Experience Stow Antiques, a cluster of stores in Stow-on-the-Wold that sell a selection of antiques and vintage goods. Explore the nooks and crannies for unusual finds and timeless treasures.

Hartley Antiques: Discover Hartley Antiques, headquartered in Chipping Campden, a shop that specializes in excellent antiques and decorative artifacts. With a choice of furniture, pottery, and artworks, it's a sanctuary for collectors.

6. Preservation of History

Antiques and vintage shops play a significant function in preserving history and tradition. By collecting these objects, you add to the conservation of craftsmanship and the stories of generations past.

7. The Joy of Discovery

Exploring antiques and vintage shops is a tour of discovery, where every corner carries the potential of unearthing a unique gem. The joy of stumbling onto a unique find is an experience that stays long after you leave the shop.

Whispers of Time

Antiques and vintage shops in the Cotswolds offer more than objects for sale; they provide whispers of time, reflections of the past that enrich the present. As you browse through these emporiums, the patina of aged wood, the rustle of vintage fabrics, and the charm of lost stories reflect the undying allure of history and nostalgia. Cotswold's antiques and vintage shops urge you to explore, to connect, and to create memories that echo the depth and history of the region.

6.3 Fashion Boutiques

Welcome to the domain of Cotswolds fashion shops, where elegance and refinement combine amidst the stunning scenery. In this part, we'll walk you through the fascination of fashion boutiques, where selected collections and distinctive designs await your discovery. From ancient classics to current trends, these boutiques offer a look into Cotswolds sartorial sophistication. Join us as we go inside stylish boutiques, examine racks of clothing, and enjoy the attraction of Cotswolds fashion scene.

1. Elegance in Every Stitch

Fashion boutiques in the Cotswolds are more than ordinary clothing stores—they are gates to luxury and self-expression. Each outfit, accessory, and design reflects the region's distinct blend of refinement and comfort.

2. Curated Collections

Experience the delight of curated sets that offer a selection of carefully chosen pieces to cater to a range of tastes. From daily staples to spectacular items, these stores pull together clothes that speak to Cotswolds unique taste.

3. Timeless Classics

Discover timeless classics that transcend trends, delivering enduring elegance that stands the test of time. Cotswold's fashion boutiques generally sell things that embody a refined sense of elegance.

4. Local Designers and Artisans

Cotswold fashion boutiques showcase local talent by presenting products from regional craftspeople and designers. These crafts offer a little originality and character to your wardrobe.

5. Exploring Cotswolds Fashion Boutiques

Boutique 3: Visit Boutique 3, located in Cheltenham, for a curated choice of women's clothes, accessories, and footwear. The store displays a blend of global and local goods.

No. 14 Boutique: Experience No. 14 Boutique in Moreton-in-Marsh, a treasure trove of contemporary women's apparel and accessories. The boutique's tasteful wares catch the essence of Cotswold elegance.

Jesse Smith: Discover Jesse Smith in Cirencester, a male boutique offering a stylish mix of clothing and accessories. With a focus on quality and flair, it's a location for discerning gentlemen.

6. Embracing Cotswolds Lifestyle

Fashion boutiques in the Cotswolds generally reflect the region's lifestyle, with selections that move effortlessly from the countryside to metropolitan surroundings. You'll find flexible outfits that fit a number of occasions.

7. Personal Styling and Service

Many Cotswold fashion businesses provide bespoke styling services, where experts help you choose pieces that suit your preferences and enhance your individual style.

The Art of Adornment

Fashion boutiques in the Cotswolds offer more than apparel; they provide the art of ornamentation, a canvas for self-expression and confidence. As you tour the stores, the delicate textures, the perfect tailoring, and the spirit of the designs match the ageless fascination of beauty and authenticity. Cotswold's fashion boutiques urge you to discover, to enjoy, and to create memories that echo the beauty and grace of the region.

6.4 Artisan Food and Drink Products

Welcome to the wonderful world of Cotswold's artisan food and drink items, where flavors and traditions meet to produce gastronomic delights. In this sector, we'll walk you through the allure of artisanal offers, where locally created goods exhibit the region's rich gastronomy. From handcrafted cheeses to small-batch preserves, these products represent the essence of Cotswolds culinary legacy. Join us as we find delightful stores, try samples, and immerse ourselves in the gourmet wealth of the Cotswolds.

1. The Craft of Flavor

Artisan food and drink products in the Cotswolds are more than sustenance—they are a celebration of flavors produced with care and affection. Each piece contains the mark of talented artisans who imbue their works with a flavor of tradition.

2. Local Ingredients

Experience the thrill of locally sourced ingredients that form the basis of handcrafted products. From honey gathered from neighboring apiaries to fruits harvested from Cotswold orchards, these elements constitute the core of the gifts.

3. Handcrafted Cheeses

Discover the charm of artisanal cheeses that represent the Cotswolds' dairy legacy. Explore a spectrum of textures and flavors, from creamy bries to pungent cheddars, each with its unique character.

4. Preserves and Condiments

Indulge in the richness of preserves and sauces that compliment your meals. From sweet jams and chutneys to zesty mustards and pickles, these commodities add layers of flavor to your culinary masterpieces.

5. Cotswold Artisan Food and Drink Shops

The Cotswold Cheese Company: Visit The Cotswold Cheese Company, a facility that offers a selection of artisan cheeses from local farmers. Sample cheeses, receive expert advice, and find the appropriate pairing.

Daylesford Organic Farm Shop: Experience Daylesford Organic Farm Shop, where you'll find a choice of organic and locally sourced food goods. Explore the shop's assortment of fresh fruit, cheeses, and handmade products.

Cotswold Food Store and Café: Discover Cotswold Food Store and Café in Moreton-in-Marsh, a haven for handcrafted items. From local cheeses to handmade chocolates, the boutique evokes the essence of Cotswold delicacies.

6. Culinary Gifts and Souvenirs

Artisan food and drink goods make for unique gifts and mementos that capture the soul of the location. Consider taking home a bit of the Cotswolds to share with loved ones.

7. Culinary Workshops and Experiences

Many artisan food and drink establishments provide classes and tasting experiences that allow you to learn about the production process and increase your enthusiasm for the goods.

A Symphony of Tastes

Artisan food and drink products in the Cotswolds give more than nutrition; they present a symphony of flavours, a trip through the flavors that distinguish the area. As you explore the shelves, the perfume of cheeses, the colours of preserves, and the stories of workmanship express the ageless fascination of food and heritage. Cotswold's artisan food and drink products allow you to taste, to appreciate, and to develop memories that represent the richness and originality of the area.

Events and Festivals

7.1 Cotswold Calendar of Events

Welcome to the exciting world of Cotswolds events and festivals, where the calendar is full with celebrations that bring the community together and urge visitors to join in the merriment. In this segment, we'll walk you through the amazing schedule of events that unfold throughout the year, each adding its unique charm to the Cotswold experience. From historic fairs to modern cultural events, these gatherings offer a look into the region's dynamic character. Join us as we discover the Cotswold calendar of activities, characterized by joy, camaraderie, and a sense of belonging.

1. Springtime Revelry

The Cotswolds come alive with a rush of springtime festivities as winter passes and nature awakens. Blossoming gardens, balmy weather, and the promise of new beginnings set the backdrop for celebrations of the season's regeneration.

Bourton-on-the-Water Model Town Open Weekend: Date: April Come to the delightful tiny town of Bourton-on-the-Water for the Bourton-on-the-Water Model Village Open Weekend. Explore carefully constructed models and enjoy the setting's quirkiness.

Lechlade Collectors' Club antique Rally & Country Show: Date: May Come celebrate antique automobiles, machinery, and rural life at the Lechlade Collectors' Club Vintage Rally & Country Show. Displays, dancing, and a nostalgic mood are all part of the celebration.

2. Summer Celebrations

Summer in the Cotswolds brings a slew of festivities that celebrate the season's warmth. Outdoor concerts, cultural exhibitions, and traditional gatherings weave together a tapestry of activities that both locals and tourists enjoy.

Cheltenham Music Festival: Date: July Enjoy the Cheltenham Music Festival, a showcase of classical music performances staged in historic venues. Immerse yourself in the melodies and abilities of world-class musicians.

Date: May Take part in the Tetbury Woolsack Races, a bizarre sport in which players sprint up and down a steep hill while carrying large sacks of wool. The competition combines athleticism with local heritage.

3. Autumn Festivities

Fall in the Cotswolds is a time for harvest festivities and intimate gatherings as the leaves change and the air becomes crisp. As the region's culinary prowess is recognized, food and drink take center stage.

Stroud Food Festival: Date: September Come to the Stroud Food Festival to see local and regional producers present their culinary delights. Explore a wide variety of culinary vendors, tastings, and cooking demonstrations.

September Indulge in the Broadway gastronomy Festival, an event that honors the gastronomy of the region. Enjoy live entertainment while sampling local dishes, handcrafted crafts, and seasonal sweets.

4. Winter Wonderland

As winter descends in the Cotswolds, the region transforms into a winter paradise, complete with Christmas lights, holiday markets, and heartwarming festivals that embrace the season's beauty.

Cheltenham Christmas Market: November-December Visit the Cheltenham Christmas Market, where wooden chalets line the streets selling homemade gifts, festive decorations, and delectable seasonal snacks.

November Visit the Cotswold Decorative, Antiques & Art Fair, a gathering of antique traders and craftspeople presenting a wide selection of collectibles, art, and vintage treasures.

A Memorable Year

The Cotswold calendar of events delivers more than just dates; it is a tapestry of experiences that highlight the region's diversity, creativity, and togetherness. As you immerse yourself in the festivities, the laughter, music, and sense of camaraderie reflect the eternal charm of tradition and community. The Cotswolds invite you to mark your calendar, enjoy the festivities, and make memories that reflect the region's depth and vibrancy.

7.2 Seasonal Celebrations

7.2.1 Cotswold Olympiads

Welcome to the vibrant world of the Cotswold Olimpick Games, a celebration that pays homage to a bygone era while injecting a modern touch. In this section, we'll look at the Cotswold Olimpick Games, a one-of-a-kind and vibrant event that pays respect to the region's heritage and passion of sport. These sports exemplify the mix of tradition and enjoyment, from fierce bouts to period costumes. Join us as we investigate the Cotswold Olimpick Games and discover the thrill of embracing tradition in a modern setting.

1. A Peek into the Past

The Cotswold Olimpick Games transport you back in time to a time when companionship, athleticism, and merriment all came together to create a remarkable spectacle. This festival, inspired by the medieval games devised by local lawyer Robert Dover in the 17th century, revives a centuries-old tradition.

2. Competitions with a Sense of Humor

Enjoy a variety of colorful competitions that capture the essence of athletics and pleasure. These games, which range from tug-of-war and shin-kicking to sack races and obstacle courses, provide a fun way to interact with history.

3. Dressing Up in Period Costumes

The opportunity to dress in period costumes and immerse yourself in the atmosphere of the past is one of the highlights of the Cotswold Olimpick Games. Dressing in traditional attire adds to the celebratory atmosphere and creates a sensation of time travel.

4. Atmosphere That Is Family-Friendly

The Cotswold Olimpick Games promote a family-friendly environment, making it an event suitable for people of all ages. Children and adults alike can participate in the various games and have a good time.

5. Each Season's Cotswold Olimpick Games

Spring Edition: Date: May Enjoy the Cotswold Olimpick Games' Spring Edition, where the rising landscapes create a backdrop for vigorous competitions and customary revelry.

Summer Edition: June Join the Cotswold Olimpick Games for the Summer Edition, when the sun-soaked surroundings come alive with laughter, friendly rivalries, and the thrill of outdoor celebrations.

Autumn Edition: Date: September Take part in the Cotswold Olimpick Games' Autumn Edition, where the changing hues of the season add to the attractiveness of the event. Accept the nostalgic atmosphere and celebrate tradition.

6. Tradition Reborn

The Cotswold Olimpick Games are more than just a series of events; they are a celebration of tradition, a means to connect with the past while adding a modern twist. By taking part, you become a part of a heritage that spans decades.

7. Accepting Community

These games give more than just competition; they promote a sense of community, a gathering place for locals and visitors to celebrate Cotswold culture and shared experiences.

The Cotswold Olimpick Games are more than just games; they are a timeless celebration, a trip through history, and sport that is relevant to today's audiences. The laughter, costumes, and camaraderie represent the enduring allure of custom and unity as you immerse yourself in the competitions. The Cotswold Olimpick Games invite you to join, enjoy, and create memories that reflect the area's depth and vibrancy.

7.2.2 Christmas Markets and Events

Welcome to the enchanting world of Cotswold Christmas markets and festivities, where the perfume of mulled wine, the sound of carolers, and the glimmer of seasonal lights fill the air. This section will immerse us in the festive mood of Christmas in the Cotswolds, where traditional markets and touching celebrations weave a tapestry of seasonal enthusiasm. These events capture the essence of the season's charm, from handcrafted goods to seasonal delicacies. Join us as we explore the Christmas markets and celebrations of the Cotswolds, a season of warmth, togetherness, and holiday cheer.

1. Splendor of the Season

Christmas in the Cotswolds is a time of festive splendor, with the region's lovely towns and villages decked out in decorations that capture the spirit of the season. Twinkling lights brighten the streets, and the aroma of roasting chestnuts fills the air.

2. Markets for Christmas

Discover the thrill of Christmas markets, which offer a treasure trove of goods, crafts, and delicacies. These markets are a refuge for holiday shoppers looking for one-of-a-kind gifts and festive treats.

3. Handmade Gifts

Discover the appeal of handcrafted goods that showcase Cotswold artists' ingenuity and expertise. From ornate ornaments to personalized jewelry, these goods are meaningful and one-of-a-kind gifts.

4. Seasonal Snacks

Enjoy the pleasures of seasonal delights that will warm your heart and please your tongue. Taste mulled wine, gingerbread, mince pies, and other festive delights associated with the holiday season.

5. Christmas Markets & Festivities in the Cotswolds

Cheltenham Christmas Market: November-December Visit the Cheltenham

Christmas Market, where wooden chalets line the streets, offering handmade items, festive decorations, and delectable seasonal snacks.

Bath Christmas Market: November-December Visit the Bath Christmas Market, which is known for its scenic location and assortment of stalls selling handmade goods, local crafts, and delicious cuisine.

November Embrace the festive environment of the Cotswold Decorative, Antiques & Art Fair, a gathering of antique traders and artisans presenting a diverse selection of antiques, art, and vintage treasures.

6. Carol Concerts and Other Forms of Entertainment

The Cotswolds' Christmas markets and festivities frequently include carol concerts, live music acts, and entertainment, which add to the festive spirit.

7. Embracing Community

The Christmas season in the Cotswolds is a time to gather with family and friends. Festivities foster a sense of community, and the warmth of shared experiences heightens the holiday spirit.

Festive Enchantment

Christmas markets and celebrations in the Cotswolds provide more than just shopping and entertainment; they bring seasonal enchantment, a chance to savour the charm of the season and make treasured memories. The laughing, the lights, and the sense of togetherness reflect the eternal charm of holiday spirit and joy as you walk through the markets, listen to carolers, and indulge in seasonal goodies. The Cotswolds beckon you to immerse yourself, to rejoice, and to create memories that reflect the area's depth and enchantment.

7.3 Festivals of Music and the Arts

Welcome to the enchanting world of Cotswold music and arts festivals, where creativity reigns supreme and melodies fill the air. In this section, we'll immerse ourselves in the vivid atmosphere of the Cotswold music and arts festivals. These festivals showcase the region's cultural wealth with fascinating performances and inspirational installations. Join us as we explore the Cotswolds' music and arts festivals, each of which is a work of art and a symphony of sensations.

1. The Inspirational Melody

Music and arts festivals in the Cotswolds are more than just events; they are gathering places for artists, musicians, and lovers to celebrate creativity in all of its manifestations.

2. Various Performances

Feel the rush of different performances that span genres and styles. From classical orchestras to modern bands, these events provide a variety of musical experiences to appeal to all tastes.

3. Visual Appeal

Discover the visual magnificence of arts events that showcase the talents of painters, sculptors, and artisans. Exhibitions, installations, and interactive displays transform locations into art galleries.

4. Workshops with an Immersive Approach

Many Cotswolds music and arts festivals provide immersive workshops where attendees may meet with artists, learn new methods, and create their own masterpieces.

5. Festivals of Music and the Arts in the Cotswolds

Cheltenham Music Festival: Date: July Enjoy the Cheltenham Music Festival, a showcase of classical music performances staged in historic venues. Immerse yourself in the melodies and abilities of world-class musicians.

Cheltenham Literature Festival: Date: October Celebrate literature at the Cheltenham Literature Festival, which features author talks, panel discussions, and book signings.

Visit the Fresh: Art Fair, an event that brings together galleries and artists to present modern art and create a platform for art fans.

6. Accepting the Experience

Attending a music or arts event in the Cotswolds is about fully immersing yourself in the experience, allowing the melodies and creativity to wash over you.

7. Improving the Experience

To maximize your enjoyment at music and arts festivals:

Plan ahead of time: Review the fair schedule and performances to guarantee you don't miss your favorite performers or exhibitions.

Immerse Yourself: To make the most of your time at the festival, interact with the artists and performers, attend workshops, and socialize with other attendees.

Bring a camera or a journal to record your favorite events and feelings, creating lasting memories.

A Creative Symphony

Music and arts festivals in the Cotswolds give more than just entertainment; they create a symphony of creation, a tapestry of melodies and pictures that represent the region's cultural wealth. The passion, colors, and spirit of invention represent the enduring fascination of artistic expression as you listen to music, tour exhibitions, and interact with artists. The Cotswolds beckon you to immerse yourself, to celebrate, and to create memories that reflect the area's depth and vibrancy.

7.4 Literary and Cultural Activities

Welcome to the Cotswolds' intellectual and cultural tapestry, where literary and cultural events weave a story of knowledge, adventure, and enlightenment. In this section, we'll look at the literary meetings and cultural festivities that help form the region's intellectual landscape. These events, ranging from author talks to heritage exhibitions, invite you to immerse yourself in stories, history, and the breadth of human expression. Join us as we explore the Cotswolds' literary and cultural events, all of which contribute to the region's ongoing story of learning and discovery.

1. A Place of Curiosity

Literary and cultural events in the Cotswolds are more than just gatherings; they are havens for inquiry, where brains meet to engage with literature, history, and thought-provoking presentations.

2. Readings and Author Talks

Discover the fascination of author lectures and readings, which offer a one-of-a-kind opportunity to engage with writers, hear their stories directly, and gain insights into the creative process.

3. Exhibitions of Cultural Heritage

Explore historical exhibitions that bring history to life by displaying items, documents, and anecdotes that shed light on the rich cultural history of the Cotswolds.

4. Discussions That Get You Thinking

Many literary and cultural events in the Cotswolds involve stimulating debates on topics ranging from literature and history to philosophy and contemporary issues.

5. Literary and Cultural Events in the Cotswolds

Cheltenham Literature Festival: Date: October Celebrate literature at the Cheltenham Literature Festival, which features author talks, panel discussions, and book signings.

Cirencester Literature Festival: Dates: October-November Celebrate the written word with presentations, seminars, and events for people of all ages at the Cirencester Literature Festival.

June Attends the Broadway Arts Festival, an event that highlights visual arts, music, and writing. In the picturesque village setting, attend exhibitions, events, and discussions.

6. Active Participation

Attending literary and cultural events in the Cotswolds entails more than just passive observation; it entails actively participating with ideas, conversations, and the area's cultural pulse.

7. Improving the Experience

To maximize your enjoyment of literary and cultural events:

Prepare: To make the most of your time, familiarize yourself with the event schedule and themes.

Engage with presenters, writers, and fellow attendees by asking questions and participating in discussions.

Network: Make relationships with like-minded people who share your interests, resulting in great conversations and connections.

Expression Chronicles

Literary and cultural events in the Cotswolds give more than intellectual stimulation; they are a mosaic of ideas and tales that build the region's cultural tapestry. The narratives, insights, and spirit of inquiry reflect the ageless attraction of knowledge and adventure as you attend author talks, explore historical exhibitions, and participate in conversations. The Cotswolds allow you to immerse yourself, study, and create experiences that reflect the area's depth and vibrancy.

Useful Information

8.1 Medical Facilities and Emergency Contacts

Welcome to the practical side of your Cotswolds adventure, where your health and safety come first. We'll give you crucial information on emergency contacts and medical facilities in this part, so you'll be ready for any unanticipated emergencies. These facts, ranging from medical services to emergency phone numbers, provide piece of mind as you explore the area. Join us as we delve into the practical knowledge that will assure your safety and comfort while visiting the Cotswolds.

1. Emergency Phone Numbers

Being prepared for crises is vital, and knowing who to call in an emergency can make all the difference.

Emergency Services (Police, Fire, Ambulance): phone: 999 (or 112) To reach the police, fire department, or ambulance services in an emergency, phone 999 or 112.

Non-Emergency Police: Dial: 101 To contact your local police station in non-emergency situations or to report a crime, dial 101.

2. Medical Services

Access to medical facilities is critical for your health, and the Cotswolds has a variety of options to make sure you're taken care of.

Local Hospitals and Medical Centers: If you require medical attention, there are various hospitals and medical centers located across the Cotswolds.

Cheltenham General Hospital: This hospital, located in Cheltenham, provides a variety of medical services.

Gloucestershire Royal Hospital: This hospital, located in Gloucester, provides extensive medical services.

Stroud General Hospital: This hospital, located in Stroud, provides medical services to the local area.

Pharmacies: Prescription drugs and over-the-counter therapies are available at local pharmacies throughout the area.

3. Insurance for Travel

Travel insurance is a wise investment because it covers unexpected medical costs, trip cancellations, and other situations. Before embarking on your journey, ensure that you have adequate coverage.

4. Keeping Healthy

Staying healthy throughout your Cotswolds journey is essential for having a good time. Stay hydrated, dress appropriately for the weather, and protect yourself from the heat by wearing sunscreen.

5. Emergencies in Medicine

In the event of a medical emergency:

Call 999 (or 112) for emergency assistance.

If you're staying in a hotel, ask the staff for guidance and support.

If possible, arrange for a local contact or friend to transport you to the medical facility.

6. Getting Ready for the Unexpected

While no one anticipates an emergency, having the right knowledge on hand can help you react quickly and effectively. Keep emergency numbers in your phone and a copy of critical contacts with you at all times.

Your well-being and safety are of the utmost importance as you embark on your Cotswolds journey. Understanding emergency contacts and medical facility locations gives you a sense of confidence, guaranteeing that you're prepared for any eventuality. The Cotswolds invite you to explore, enjoy, and make memories while keeping your safety in mind.

8.2 Banking and Currency Services

Welcome to the practical side of your Cotswolds vacation, where understanding money and banking services guarantees easy financial transactions. In this section, we'll teach you about the local currency, banking services, and how to handle your finances while touring the area. From currency exchange to ATM locations, these data are useful as you travel through the Cotswolds. Join us as we delve into the practical knowledge that will assure your financial comfort during your Cotswolds adventure.

1. The local currency

The British Pound Sterling (£) is the primary currency in the Cotswolds, as it is throughout the United Kingdom. To facilitate transactions, it is recommended that you become acquainted with the denominations and currency symbols.

2. Banking Services

The Cotswolds provides a variety of banking services to meet your financial needs.

Banks and Branches: The Cotswolds' major towns and villages all have banks and branches where you can undertake various banking transactions.

ATMs (Cash Machines): ATMs, often known as cash machines, are common across the Cotswolds. They make it simple to withdraw cash in local currency using your debit or credit card.

3. Currency Conversion

You can exchange foreign currency for British pounds at banks, currency exchange offices, and select post offices. Currency conversion rates might vary, so it's best to compare them before making any purchases.

4. Payment Options

Major credit and debit cards are widely accepted in Cotswolds stores, restaurants, and hotels. However, for smaller locations that may not accept cards, it's always a good idea to have some cash.

5. Managing Your Money

While traveling through the Cotswolds, keep the following in mind:

Inform Your Bank: Notify your bank of your travel plans to avoid having your cards stopped due to odd behavior.

Online Banking: Many hotels include complimentary Wi-Fi, allowing you to conduct online banking and keep track of transactions.

Security precautions: Always keep your credit cards, cash, and critical papers secure.

6. Apps for Converting Currency

Currency conversion applications are useful tools for swiftly converting quantities from your own currency to British Pounds. They can be useful for predicting costs and making educated decisions.

Financial Ease is the conclusion.

Knowing currency and banking services as you begin on your Cotswolds excursion ensures financial simplicity throughout your journey. The Cotswolds allow you to explore and enjoy the region while being financially aware and prepared, whether you're withdrawing cash, making card payments, or managing your accounts online.

8.3 Internet and Communication Services

Welcome to the modern era of your Cotswolds vacation, where being connected via communication and internet services improves your overall experience. We'll give you crucial information regarding mobile networks, internet access, and ways to interact with loved ones while touring the region in this section. These things, from remaining online to making phone calls, provide ease and connectivity during your Cotswolds holiday. Join us as we delve into the practical facts that will keep you in touch with the world around you.

1. Cellular Networks

Major mobile networks cover the Cotswolds, allowing you to stay connected wherever you go.

2. Local Numbers and SIM Cards

If you're going from another country and intend to use your phone regularly, consider buying a local

SIM card. This gives you a local phone number and access to local rates.

3. Internet Connection

The internet is generally available across the Cotswolds, making it simple to remain connected and share your experiences.

Wi-Fi Hotspots: Many hotels, cafes, restaurants, and public spaces provide free Wi-Fi to its guests and visitors.

4G Coverage: Major cities and towns typically offer great 4G coverage, allowing you to use mobile data for a variety of online activities.

4. Apps for Communication

Apps like WhatsApp, Skype, and FaceTime are great for staying in touch with family and friends back home. You can make voice and video calls through the internet, saving money on international calls.

5. Emergency Notifications

Local officials send out emergency alerts to the majority of cell phones. These notifications can provide critical information in the event of a natural disaster, an emergency, or a safety notice.

6. International Travel

Check with your cell network provider about international roaming prices and packages before using your phone abroad. This can help you avoid unanticipated expenditures.

7. Maintain Your Presence

While it is crucial to stay connected, remember to balance your online connections with the beauty and tranquility of the Cotswolds. Take some time to disconnect and truly immerse yourself in the natural surroundings.

Staying connected with phone and internet services while on your Cotswolds vacation adds convenience to your journey. The Cotswolds encourage you to explore, interact, and find a perfect balance between the digital and natural worlds, whether you're sharing your experiences with friends and family or utilizing maps to navigate.

8.4 Language and Cultural Practices

Welcome to the Cotswolds' world of language and local customs, where grasping the nuances of communication and cultural etiquette enriches your relationships with people. In this section, you'll learn about the language spoken, social standards, and rituals that create the Cotswold way of life. These subtleties, ranging from greetings to etiquette, provide a greater knowledge of the region's culture. Join us as we investigate the practical facts that will enhance your cultural experience while visiting the Cotswolds.

1. Language Used

The predominant language spoken in the Cotswolds is English. However, you may encounter accents and dialects that contribute to the beauty of your interactions with locals.

2. Greetings and Social Expectations

Understanding local greetings and social conventions can help you interact with the community in a courteous manner.

When meeting someone, a simple "Hello" or "Hi" is sufficient. A warm smile and eye contact can go a long way toward generating a good first impression.

Politeness: Politeness is very important. "Please" and "Thank you" are fundamental etiquette and appreciation phrases.

3. Punctuality

Being on time for meetings and gatherings demonstrates respect for the time of others.

4. Tipping

In restaurants and cafes, tipping is customary. While not obligatory, a tip of roughly 10-15% of the total is appreciated for excellent service.

5. The Dress Code

The Cotswolds are known for their casual and easygoing dress code. Smart-casual dress is appropriate for dining at fancier restaurants or attending cultural activities.

6. Public Conduct

Respecting public areas and acting considerately are essential. Avoid littering, obey all signs, and obey all regulations.

7. Local Traditions and Festivals

Participating in local festivals and rituals provides a unique perspective on Cotswold life. Take part in the festivities, enjoy the events, and interact with the community.

8. Accept the Experience

Immersing oneself in local customs and etiquette allows you to engage with the Cotswold culture on a deeper level. Be willing to learn and adapt to the local ways.

Cultural Links

Understanding language and local customs increases your cultural experience in the Cotswolds, building relationships and meaningful encounters with locals. You become a part of the Cotswold community by obeying social norms, adopting customs, and engaging in respectful behavior, enriching your adventure with authenticity and depth.

8.5 Special Needs Travelers' Accessibility

Welcome to the inclusive portion of your Cotswolds vacation, where accessibility for tourists with special needs guarantees that everyone may comfortably explore the area. This section will offer you with crucial information regarding facilities, services, and considerations for disabled tourists. From accessible lodgings to transit options, these elements provide a warm welcome to all visitors.

Join us as we delve into the practical information that supports inclusive exploration during your trip to the Cotswolds.

1. Accommodations for the Disabled

The Cotswolds provide a variety of accessible accommodations.

Many hotels, inns, and bed-and-breakfast places include accessible rooms with amenities such as larger doorways, roll-in showers, and grab bars.

Reservations for Accommodation: When making reservations, inform the establishment of your accessibility requirements to ensure that appropriate accommodations are made.

2. Transportation

Accessible transportation options make it easier to get about the Cotswolds.

Public Transportation: Buses and railways frequently offer amenities to assist disabled passengers. Look for information about accessible routes and services.

Private Transportation: For more comfortable travel, consider reserving private transportation providers that have accessible cars.

3. Attractions and Services

Many Cotswold sites and facilities are designed to be accessible.

Historic Sites: Some historic sites have easily accessible trails and facilities, allowing everyone to appreciate their beauty and history.

Museums and Galleries: Many museums and galleries have accessible entrances, ramps, and elevators to promote inclusive exploration.

Restaurants and Cafés: To ensure a comfortable dining experience, look for venues with ramps, wider aisles, and accessible seating.

4. Assistance and Information

Tourist information centers and hotels are frequently eager to assist guests with particular needs.

Local Knowledge: Seek information on accessible venues, facilities, and services from local resources.

5. Preparation is essential.

Travelers with special needs must plan ahead of time to ensure a smooth and pleasurable vacation.

Before your vacation, look into the accessibility of your chosen locations and hotels.

Communication: If you have specific requirements, don't be afraid to communicate them to lodging providers, tour operators, and other relevant parties.

6. Accept Inclusion

The Cotswolds are dedicated to providing an all-inclusive experience for all visitors. By encouraging inclusive exploration, you contribute to a more accessible and friendly environment.

Comprehensive Exploration

Understanding accessibility for tourists with special needs as you begin your Cotswolds journey guarantees that everyone may enjoy the region's beauty and charm. By selecting accessible accommodations, taking use of transportation choices, and visiting attractions designed with inclusiveness in mind, you become a member of the Cotswold community, which embraces diversity and gives opportunity for everyone to explore, enjoy, and create lasting experiences.

Tourism Official Websites and Information Centers

Welcome to the chapter on handy gadgets that will accompany you on your Cotswolds adventure. We'll give you crucial information about official tourism websites and local information centers that will serve as your guides to the area in this part. These details provide you with a plethora of information to help your exploration, ranging from online tools to in-person guidance. Join us as we delve into the practical knowledge that will connect you with the Cotswolds' heart.

1. Tourism Official Websites

Visit The Cotswolds (www.visitthecotswolds.org.uk): The Cotswolds' major tourism website provides a variety of information about sights, lodgings, events, and practical travel tips. Explore it to plan your trip and learn about the region's offerings.

Cotswolds Area of Outstanding Natural Beauty (www.cotswoldsaonb.org.uk): The Cotswolds Area of Outstanding Natural Beauty website provides detailed information about the region's natural landscapes, trails, and conservation initiatives. It is an excellent resource for outdoor enthusiasts.

2. Local Resource Centers

Local information centers provide specialized advice and information to visitors to the Cotswolds.

Cirencester Tourist Information Centre: This center, located in Cirencester, provides brochures, maps, and expert advice to help you make the most of your visit.

Cheltenham Tourist Information Centre: This center in Cheltenham provides information on area sights, events, and lodging.

Stroud Tourist Information Centre: Located in Stroud, this center provides information on local attractions, walks, and cultural experiences.

3. Maps and visitor guides

Maps and visitor guides are necessary for touring the Cotswolds.

Printed Guides: Many tourist information centers sell printed guides with maps, suggested itineraries, and information about local attractions.

Explore online maps that highlight attractions, trails, lodging, and other points of interest.

4. Apps for Traveling

Travel apps put convenience at your fingertips.

Visit The Cotswolds App: For convenient access to information, maps, and suggested routes, download the official Cotswolds app.

Google Maps: Use Google Maps to travel and discover the roads, trails, and attractions of the Cotswolds.

5. Social networking sites

To stay up to current on events, promotions, and local insights, follow official Cotswolds tourism accounts on social media sites.

Finally, your Cotswolds companions

Official tourist websites, local information centers, maps, and apps become excellent companions as you travel around the Cotswolds, guiding you through the region's attractions. These resources ensure that you have the knowledge and insights needed for an enriching and memorable vacation, whether you're looking for accommodations, planning routes, or discovering hidden gems.

Travel Forums and Communities Online

Welcome to the virtual world of online travel forums and communities that bring visitors together. This section will give you with important information on internet platforms where you may interact with other explorers, share experiences, and gain crucial ideas for your Cotswolds adventure. These sites provide a network of like-minded individuals who are passionate about travel, from seeking guidance to sharing memories. Join us as we delve into the practical information that will connect you to a network of like-minded adventurers.

1. TripAdvisor (www.tripadvisor.com): TripAdvisor is a popular platform where travelers post reviews, recommendations, and information on Cotswolds attractions, lodgings, restaurants, and more. It's a great place to obtain ideas from other travelers.

2. Thorn Tree Forum (www.lonelyplanet.com/thorntree): The Thorn Tree Forum is a section of Lonely Planet's website where travelers can ask questions, exchange experiences, and offer assistance. It's a terrific place to meet other travellers and learn about the Cotswolds.

3. Reddit Travel Community (www.reddit.com/r/travel): The Reddit travel

community is a forum where travelers may discuss various destinations, including the Cotswolds. You may ask questions, share experiences, and get advice from other redditors.

4. Facebook Travel Groups: There are various travel groups on Facebook where you can join discussions about the Cotswolds, ask for assistance, and interact with other travelers.

Cotswolds Travel Group: A group of travelers who share their opinions and experiences regarding visiting the Cotswolds.

Connect with other lone travelers for advice and camaraderie during your trip.

5. Local Forums: Cotswolds-specific forums provide perspectives from residents and frequent visitors.

Cotswold Forum (www.cotswoldforum.com): Participate in conversations regarding many facets of the Cotswolds, such as attractions and local events.

6. Participate and contribute

Participating in online travel networks and groups is a two-way street.

Inquire: Don't be afraid to inquire about the Cotswolds, whether it's about attractions, accommodations, or travel recommendations.

Share Your Experiences: After your Cotswolds excursion, share your thoughts, comments, and insights with future visitors.

As you plan your vacation to the Cotswolds, internet travel forums and groups will become your virtual travel family. Connecting with other travelers, exchanging tales, and asking advice adds a sense of community to your journey. By participating in debates, you contribute to a community reservoir of knowledge that helps travelers discover the beauty and charm of the Cotswolds.

Itineraries Examples

9.1 Itinerary for a Weekend Getaway

Welcome to the sample itineraries that will help you plan your Cotswolds vacation. In this section, we'll walk you through a weekend trip plan that will allow you to discover the spirit of the Cotswolds in just two days. This schedule guarantees that you make the most of your limited time by seeing attractive communities and historic sites. Join us as we delve into the practical facts that will guide you through a wonderful Cotswolds weekend.

Itinerary for a Weekend Getaway to the Cotswolds in Two Days

Day 1: Visit Historic Villages

Bourton-on-the-Water in the morning

Begin your day in the scenic town of Bourton-on-the-Water, known as the "Venice of the Cotswolds." Stroll down the peaceful River

Windrush, cross its charming stone bridges, and visit traditional tea cafes and local stores. The Cotswold Motoring Museum, which has historic cars and nostalgic displays, is not to be missed.

Lunch with A Typical Pub Experience

A classic Cotswold lunch can be had at a nearby pub. Enjoy hearty dishes like pie and mash with a local ale. Stow-on-the-Wold in the afternoon Stow-on-the-Wold, a medieval market town noted for its market square and antique stores, is a must-see. Explore St. Edward's Church and its magnificent structure. Wander through the streets surrounded with charming buildings and visit the local stores.

Sunset at Broadway Tower in the evening

Drive to the Broadway Tower, a well-known Cotswold landmark. As the sun sets, take in panoramic views of the rolling hills and rivers.

Day 2: Cultural Enchantments and Natural Beauty

Sudeley Castle in the morning

Begin your day visiting Sudeley Castle, which is rich in history and set amid lovely grounds. Explore the interiors of the castle, which are steeped in Tudor and Victorian history. Enjoy the tranquillity by taking a leisurely stroll through the award-winning gardens.

Riverside Picnic Lunch

Pack a picnic and head to one of the peaceful areas in the Cotswolds, such as the banks of the River Windrush. As you eat, take in the beauty of nature. Cotswold Hills & Walks in the Afternoon. Take a stroll across the Cotswold Hills. The Cotswold Way National Trail has several paths that suit to different levels of fitness. Choose a suitable track and enjoy the panoramic views and lovely sceneries.

Evening: Farewell and Local Cuisine

Indulge in a delectable dinner at a nearby restaurant, savoring Cotswold cuisine crafted with fresh, local ingredients. Finally, it was a memorable weekend.

This weekend vacation plan highlights the appeal of the Cotswolds, from historic towns and cultural attractions to magnificent natural beauty. While two days may seem short, this plan guarantees you see the attractions of the region, leaving you with fond memories and a desire to return for more Cotswolds adventure.

9.2 Week-Long Excursions

Welcome to a week-long exploration plan that allows you to immerse yourself in the beauty and variety of the Cotswolds. In this section, we'll lay up a seven-day plan for you to explore the region's medieval villages, natural landscapes, cultural sites, and more. This itinerary provides a comprehensive Cotswolds experience, from quaint towns to magnificent homes. Join us as we delve into the details that will guide you through a great week in the Cotswolds.

Itinerary for a Weeklong Exploration of the Cotswolds

Day 1: Arrival and Orientation

Arrive in Cirencester in the afternoon.

Begin your week at the medieval market town of Cirencester. Explore the town center, pay a visit to the Corinium Museum, and learn about Cotswold history.

Afternoon: Welcome Dinner

Indulge in regional flavors during a welcome supper at a local restaurant.

Day 2: Natural Beauty and Historic Villages

Bibury in the morning

Visit Bibury, which is famous for its lovely Arlington Row residences. Visit the Trout Farm and explore the gorgeous surroundings.

Cotswold Wildlife Park in the afternoon

Spend time at Cotswold Wildlife Park, which has a wide variety of animals and gorgeous grounds.

Day 3: Stately Residences and Gardens

Blenheim Palace in the morning

Visit the UNESCO World Heritage Site of Blenheim Palace. Investigate the grand castle interiors, beautiful gardens, and ancient parkland.

Shopping in Bicester Village in the afternoon

Take a break from shopping in Bicester Village, an outlet mall with designer retailers.

Day 4 Cultural Delights and Culinary Adventures

Cheltenham in the morning

Explore Cheltenham's cultural offerings, which include museums, galleries, and fine architecture.

Cooking Class and Tea Tasting in the Afternoon

Take a Cotswold cooking lesson to learn how to make traditional foods. Then proceed with a tea tasting lesson.

Day 5: Exploring Nature and Local Artists

Cotswold Water Park in the morning

Spend the morning exploring the tranquil lakes and wildlife areas of the Cotswold Water Park.

Afternoon: Visit Local Artist Studios

Visit local artisan workshops and studios to learn about craftsmanship firsthand.

Day 6: Villages and Countryside Walks

Cotswold Way Trail in the Morning

Enjoy panoramic vistas as you walk along a section of the Cotswold Way National Trail.

Moreton-in-Marsh in the afternoon

Moreton-in-Marsh is a medieval market town with beautiful streets and local markets.

Day 7: Goodbye to the Cotswolds

Sudeley Castle and Gardens in the morning

Return to Sudeley Castle for a more in-depth look at its history and gardens.

Afternoon: Departure and Farewell Lunch

Enjoy a farewell meal at a local restaurant before departing, relishing your final minutes in the Cotswolds.

A Week to Remember

This weeklong exploration plan takes you through the unique tapestry of history, nature, culture, and gastronomy that is the Cotswolds. From ancient monuments and stately homes to picturesque hikes and artisan encounters, this itinerary will leave you with a profound appreciation for the Cotswolds and a collection of treasured experiences.

9.3 Activities for the Whole Family

Welcome to the program of family-friendly activities that will provide unique experiences for everyone in your party. In this section, we'll give you a thorough itinerary packed with exciting and engaging activities appropriate for families with children. This schedule guarantees that everyone in the family has a good time in the Cotswolds, from interactive attractions to outdoor experiences. Join us as we delve into the practical knowledge that will assist you in planning a fun family vacation.

Itinerary of Family-Friendly Activities: Memorable Moments for All Ages

Day 1: Arrival and Orientation

Arrive in Cheltenham in the afternoon.

Start your family vacation in Cheltenham. After your excursion, unwind with a leisurely stroll in Montpellier Gardens.

Evening: Dinner with Family

Enjoy a family dinner at a nearby restaurant with a children's menu and a relaxing atmosphere.

Day 2: Nature and Wildlife

Cotswold Wildlife Park in the morning

Begin your day with a stroll around Cotswold Wildlife Park, where children may observe creatures from all over the world. Picnic at Birdland Park and Gardens in the afternoon

Picnic at Birdland Park and Gardens, where you may encounter exotic birds and relax in magnificent outdoor spaces.

Day 3: Village Discovery and Adventure

Bourton-on-the-Water in the morning

Discover the Model Village and experience family-friendly attractions in Bourton-on-the-Water.

Cotswold Motoring Museum in the afternoon

The Cotswold Motoring Museum, which features vintage cars and interactive exhibits, will captivate young brains.

Day 4: Exploration and Creativity

Family Pottery Workshop in the Morning

Participate in a family pottery workshop where everyone may express themselves through clay.

Afternoon: Visit Sudeley Castle.

Discover Sudeley Castle's family-friendly amenities, from its exhibitions to its gorgeous grounds.

Day 5: Outdoor Activities

Puzzling Adventure Trail in the Morning

Set out on a family-friendly adventure route, solving riddles and learning about your surroundings.

Cotswold Farm Park in the afternoon

Spend the afternoon at Cotswold Farm Park, where children can interact with animals and play in outdoor spaces.

Day 6: Active Investigation

Cotswold Archery and Bushcraft in the Morning

In an exciting outdoor session, you may try your hand at archery and learn bushcraft techniques.

Cycling with the family in the afternoon

Rent bikes and embark on a family riding adventure along scenic paths or through charming communities.

Day 7: Goodbye to Family Memories

Morning: Cattle Country Adventure Park's Magic

Cattle Country Adventure Park, with farm animals and play areas, will enchant you.

Afternoon: Departure and Farewell Picnic

Before leaving the Cotswolds, enjoy a goodbye picnic in a nearby park.

Family Relationships and Adventures

This program of family-friendly activities allows you to bond, discover, and make precious memories together. The Cotswolds offer a playground for all ages, from wildlife encounters to artistic workshops and outdoor excursions, ensuring that your family trip is packed with joy, laughter, and the spirit of adventure.

Travel and Photography Tips

10.1 Capturing the Beauty of the Cotswolds

Welcome to the chapter of photography and travel ideas to help you get the most out of your Cotswolds adventure through the lens of your camera. In this section, we'll provide you tips and techniques for capturing the beauty and charm of the Cotswolds in your photography. These techniques can help you create unique photographs that truly capture the character of the location, from breathtaking landscapes to lovely villages. Join us as we delve into the practical information that will help you improve your photography in the Cotswolds.

1. Accept Golden Hours

Make the most of the "golden hours," the period of time between sunrise and sunset when the light is mellow and pleasant. These magnificent moments illuminate the Cotswold landscapes, increasing the splendor of the towns and countryside.

2. Architecture Framing

The architecture of the Cotswolds is a visual feast. Make use of the gorgeous houses, stone walls, and old structures as natural framing for your photographs. Experiment with different perspectives to capture their own personality.

3. Capture Specifics

Don't only concentrate on the big shots. Zoom in to capture fine details such as cobblestone streets, blooming flowers, and rustic signs. These elements give your Cotswolds photo collection depth and authenticity.

4. Investigate Symmetry

Look for symmetrical compositions, such as reflections in still bodies of water or perfectly lined rows of trees. Photographs with symmetry can be visually beautiful and balanced.

5. Experiment with Depth of Field

Experiment with depth of field by creating a narrow depth of field using a wide aperture (low f-number). This blurs the background, allowing your subject to be plainly visible.

6. Capture Seasonal Variations

Visit the Cotswolds at different times of year to experience the region's ever-changing splendor. Spring delivers colorful blooms, summer brings lush vegetation, fall brings warm hues, and winter brings coziness.

7. Observe Local Life

Engage with people and take candid photos of their daily lives in the Cotswolds. These images communicate stories, whether they depict a market scene or a friendly conversation.

8. Cotswold Hills Sunrise

Climb a hill in the early morning to see the dawn over the Cotswold Hills. The panoramic view, bathed in warm morning light, offers spectacular photo opportunities.

9. Investigate Different Points of View

Experiment with different points of view and viewpoints. To add variation to your collection, take photos from high vantage points, via archways, or beneath blooming trees.

10. Respect and a Request for Permission

Respect people's privacy when shooting them, especially in cities. Ask for permission before snapping photographs. Building rapport might result in more authentic and comfortable emotions.

Telling Stories Through Your Lens

Remember that each photograph tells a story as you travel around the Cotswolds with your camera in hand. Your photographs generate visual narratives that highlight the beauty and soul of the Cotswolds, whether it's the charm of a town, the tranquillity of nature, or the warmth of local relationships. Using these photography suggestions, you'll be able to build a collection of photographs that not only exhibit the beauties of the place, but also represent the emotions and memories you've had while your trip.

10.2 Travel Photography Practices That Are Respectful

Welcome to the section of respectful travel photography practices that will help you capture the beauty of the Cotswolds while also respecting the people and places that live there. In this section, we'll provide you vital tips on how to approach photography with mindfulness and consideration. From interacting with locals to protecting cultural assets, these methods ensure that your photography adventure contributes positively to the ecosystem of the Cotswolds. Join us as we go into the practical aspects of respectful photography.

1. Request Permission

When shooting individuals, especially in intimate settings, always ask for permission first. Respect their privacy and wishes, and engage in nice conversation before photographing them.

2. Keep Cultural Sensitivities in Mind

Respect the local traditions and customs. When photographing religious ceremonies, sacred sites, or cultural activities, exercise caution. It's preferable to observe discreetly and avoid snapping photographs if possible.

3. Participate in Conversations

Make friends with the people you shoot. Engage in conversation, learn about their life, and demonstrate genuine interest. This not only improves your experience, but it also results in more authentic and meaningful photographs.

4. Prevent Disruptive Behavior

Avoid disruptive behavior in congested locations or places of worship that could irritate the residents or the atmosphere. When taking images, keep a reasonable distance and limit distractions.

5. Natural Environments Should Be Preserved

Respect the environment when photographing natural scenery. To avoid harming vulnerable ecosystems, stay on identified pathways. Avoid upsetting wildlife and leaving no trace of your presence.

6. Private Spaces Must Be Respected

Remember that many dwellings in villages and towns are private residences. Without permission, do not photograph people's homes or lawns. If you're curious about a particular structure, inquire before photographing it.

7. Use Caution in Highly Sensitive Areas

Some areas may be considered sensitive due to privacy concerns or historical value. Use your discretion to determine if it is appropriate to take photographs. When in doubt, seek guidance.

8. Tell Your Story

Provide context and convey the story behind your images when sharing them online or with others. This gives depth to the shot and aids others in understanding the cultural significance.

9. Give Something Back

Consider donating to the locations you picture. Support local businesses, artists, and programs that benefit the community.

10. Inform Yourself

Before going anywhere, learn about its history, culture, and etiquette. Understanding the context will assist you in approaching photography with compassion and respect.

Respectful travel photography is a way to pay tribute to the people and places you encounter. You may produce a collection of images that not only showcase the beauty of the Cotswolds but also reflect your respect for its citizens and history by practicing mindfulness, seeking permission, and engaging in meaningful conversations. Through your lens, you become a storyteller who captures true moments, increasing your own experience and positively contributing to the area.

10.3 Ideas for a Memorable Cotswolds Vacation

Welcome to the chapter of tips to make your trip to the Cotswolds more enjoyable, enjoyable, and memorable. In this section, we'll give you crucial insights and guidance to help you explore the region's offerings, from attractions to local customs. These hints are your valued companions, assisting you in making the most of your time in the Cotswolds. Join us as we delve into the practical knowledge that will benefit you in every aspect on your path.

1. Make a Plan

Prepare by researching the attractions, lodgings, and transportation options in the Cotswolds. Planning allows you to make the most of your time and have a pleasant experience.

2. Pack for Unpredictable Weather

The weather in the Cotswolds can be unpredictable. Pack layers, waterproof clothing, walking shoes, and don't forget an umbrella.

3. Accept Slow Travel

The appeal of the Cotswolds lies in their leisurely pace. Slow travel allows you to properly appreciate the area's beauty and culture.

4. Interact with Locals

Interact with locals to learn about their way of life and to obtain insider information. Engaging conversations lead to genuine connections.

5. Local customs must be followed.

Learn about the local customs and manners. Simple behaviors such as saying "please" and "thank you" go a long way toward demonstrating respect.

6. Taste the Local Cuisine

Local cafes and traditional taverns serve Cotswold cuisine. Don't pass up the opportunity to explore regional dishes and local favorites.

7. Mindfully Capture Memories

Be mindful of people's privacy and cultural sensitivity when taking images. When photographing people, always obtain permission first.

8. Investigate Off-the-Beaten-Path

While prominent attractions should not be missed, lesser-known communities and trails should also be explored. These hidden treasures provide one-of-a-kind experiences.

9. Allow for Unpredictability

Make place in your agenda for spontaneity. Some of the most incredible events occur when you least expect them.

10. Help Local Businesses

Shop at local markets, boutiques, and artisan stores. Supporting local businesses benefits both the economy and cultural preservation in the region.

11. Travel in a Sustainable Manner

Respect the environment by practicing environmentally responsible travel. Reduce your waste, stay in eco-friendly accommodations, and leave no trace.

12. Stay Safe and Connected

Make certain that you have access to communication and computing services. Save emergency contact information and stay up to date on local safety regulations.

13. Seasonal Events to Attend

Check the calendar for yearly events, festivals, and fairs in the Cotswolds. Attending these events allows you to learn about local customs and society.

14. Immerse yourself in nature.

Take advantage of the natural beauty of the Cotswolds. Take walks, hikes, or simply spend time in peaceful locations to recharge your batteries.

15. Develop Curiosity

Be interested in the history and tales of the landmarks and attractions. Knowing more about the location will enhance your whole experience.

Begin a Meaningful Journey

By following these suggestions, you will embark on a trip that goes beyond regular travel. Your Cotswolds experience develops a tapestry of connections, insights, and experiences that influence your recollections for years to come, from connecting with people to actively collecting memories. As you tour this wonderful location, may these suggestions serve as a guiding light, improving every aspect of your journey.

Finally, begin your Cotswolds adventure.

Congratulations! You've read the entire "Cotswolds Travel Guide," which is your go-to guide for exploring this wonderful region. You now have a plethora of knowledge at your fingertips to ensure a wonderful journey, from historic villages to stately homes, stunning landscapes to cultural excursions. As you prepare to embark on your Cotswolds journey, here's a quick recap to round up your research:

The Introduction sets the tone for your trip, introducing you to the ageless beauty, rich history, and beautiful scenery of the Cotswolds. It's a place that begs you to become lost in its beauty and sincerity.

Planning Your Trip provides you with the knowledge you need to organize a successful trip. From the best time to visit to recommended lengths of stay and modes of transportation, you'll find practical guidance to ensure your trip is personalized to your tastes.

The Top Attractions section transports you to medieval villages, magnificent homes, natural landscapes, and artistic expressions. Each component provides detailed information about major destinations, assisting you in prioritizing your experiences.

Outdoor Activities encourages you to enjoy the natural beauty of the Cotswolds through hiking, cycling, horseback riding, and other activities. This section has you covered if you're an outdoor enthusiast or looking for family-friendly excursions.

Local Cuisine and Dining welcomes you to sample the gastronomic delights of the Cotswolds. You'll discover the region's gastronomic gems, from traditional pubs to fine dining venues, tea rooms to farmers' markets.

Souvenirs, local crafts, antiques, fashion, and artisan culinary products abound in the Cotswolds. The Cotswolds' shopping scene awaits, whether you're looking for souvenirs or one-of-a-kind gifts.

The section Events and Festivals provides a schedule of annual events such as seasonal festivals, music and arts celebrations, and literary activities. Participate in these exciting gatherings to immerse yourself in the colorful culture of the Cotswolds.

Practical Information provides you with important information such as emergency contacts, currencies, communication services, local customs, accessibility, and more, guaranteeing a smooth and trouble-free vacation.

Useful Resources links you to government tourism websites, online travel forums, and communities where you may obtain more information and interact with other tourists.

The Sample Itineraries section caters to various travel types and interests by providing weekend getaways, weeklong explorations, family-friendly activities, and photographic ideas.

In the end, visiting the Cotswolds is about more than just checking off sites; it's about embracing the region's character, interacting with its people, and creating lasting memories. The Cotswolds has something special to offer every tourist, whether they are captivated by the medieval villages, enthralled by the beautiful vistas, or charmed by the local culture.

As you go on your tour, keep an open heart, an inquiring mind, and a respect for the region's history in mind. The Cotswolds will warmly welcome you, and your discovery will become a treasured part of your travel tale. So pack your luggage, begin your adventure, and let the Cotswolds work its magic on your soul.

Safe travels and joyful Cotswolds adventures!

© **Rick Paul**

Made in the USA
Las Vegas, NV
13 December 2023